Dedication

To both our families. Thank you for the hat trick.

Contents

Contents

List of figures

Acknowledgements

This book is a distillation of many hours of learning, listening, reading, practising, teaching, and talking about communication with many past and present colleagues and students. We owe debts directly and indirectly to more people and places than we realize for stimulating ideas and activities over many years. We have been, and are, fortunate in experiencing the excitement of working with colleagues who are committed to teaching communication.

We are also fortunate to have forbearing families who have been prepared to tolerate evenings, weekends and 'holidays' which have been preoccupied with researching and writing another book. So our special thanks to Maggie, Tom and Lottie, and to Gill, Nick and Caroline for reminding us that teaching is only 'work' and writing only a 'hobby'.

We and our publishers would also like to thank those listed below for their permission to reproduce copyright material: for extracts from syllabi – the AEB, the SEG, the NEA, the LCCI, the RSA, the University of Cambridge Local Examinations Syndicate, the City and Guilds of London Institute, BTEC; for birthday cards – Andrew Valentine, Giesen and Wolf Ltd., Peverel Cards, Raphael Tuck, Wilson Brothers Greeting Cards Ltd. Every effort has been made to trace all copyright holders: our apologies to those in cases where this has not proved possible.

Introduction

Our aim is to provide practical information about teaching communication in schools and in post-compulsory education and training. We are seeking to identify a clearly laid out schema of what teaching communication means in practice.

The need to enable young people consciously to develop 'communication skills' is now firmly established – it can rest on a purely functional base and is often labelled 'English' or 'social and life skills' as well as 'communication'. We agree with that. But we want to go further.

First, in addition to learning 'skills', we believe that studying communication is about the personal development of attitudes and values; about knowing oneself; about knowing other people and relating to them; about critically understanding mass-media messages; and about being confident in the use of communication technologies.

Second, teaching communication is not about learning the requisite linguistic and social skills in isolation, like a series of performing tricks, but about acquiring knowledge of how and why we communicate and about the application of that knowledge.

Communicative competence in our life roles – personal, social and economic – is founded on our knowledge about social, cultural and economic contexts. It depends on using and applying that knowledge.

Third, in a school or college context the idea of communication skills still has the notion of something basic for the less able, something that can be left for the more able student to 'pick up'. We believe that all pupils and students should be deliberately exposed to some of the experiences and activities that we describe in this book as 'communication work'.

We enjoy being teachers of communication (most of the time!) since it provides a constant flow of new ideas and experiences. We hope that some of our enjoyment will be shared with you through this book.

A note on the organization of this book

It may be helpful to add a word of explanation about why we have arranged things as they are so that you can find your way round the book more easily. Chapter 1 outlines the assumptions, general aims and current ideas which we consider to be significant in the teaching of communication. We recommend that Chapters 2 and 3 are read together, since the 'what' and 'how' of teaching are clearly inseparable. 'The medium is the message' as we used to be urged to think by the late Marshall McLuhan. He was right, of course, but he took the notion too far for most people. In our case we felt that it was preferable to state what is being taught in simple descriptive terms without analysis, and to flesh this out with some sample course plans. These work schemes are not intended as models for you to follow, but rather as a particular approach that you can change to suit your own aims, needs and circumstances. In Chapter 3 we have sought to analyse and exemplify some of the issues and strategies of teaching that we have found useful.

Chapter 4 provides examples of teaching materials. It is a collection of resource ideas that you can use or adapt, such as introductory exercises, discussion/group-work topics; criteria by which to judge 'effective' communication; case studies and role plays; a sequence on advertising; a semiotic analysis of everyday objects; and a guide to finding your way round the library classification.

Chapter 5 provides a summary of some communication syllabuses available in the UK. A selection of resources and sources of information for teachers can be found in Chapter 6. Finally, in Chapter 7 we outline how the study of communication can be helpful in a variety of careers, and how it can be pursued at a variety of higher education institutions.

Graeme Burton
Richard Dimbleby
October 1988

Chapter one

What about communication?

This book is small but ambitious. It will deal with communication (including media) teaching in a wide range of situations, as taught by a diversity of teachers. We believe that we can take this approach precisely because communication work in all areas does have a great deal in common, whatever the syllabus or terms of reference. Indeed, one of the purposes of this book is to make this common ground apparent, to bring us all together.

Our audience

You may be working with students of very different abilities and interests, in a wide range of institutions, or preparing to teach for the first time, but we hope that we have something to say about how communication may be taught which will be useful to all of you. This means that we are addressing those whose main interest is media studies, as well as those in communication work. It means that we are saying something to school teachers dealing with TVE or CPVE, and for FE teachers working with BTEC courses or other pre-vocational work. We address ourselves to GCE and GCSE teachers alike. And we hope that colleagues in polytechnics will also find something of value here. Certainly we hope that those being trained as teachers will want to read this book, and that we can introduce them to new concepts, new approaches, and a new subject.

In fact communication (or communication studies) is not so new any more. The first A-level examination was held in 1978, and degrees in the subject have been running for well over a decade. Communication work in a pre-vocational context at all levels has expanded enormously in the 1980s, with new syllabuses and forms of assessment significantly affected by the creation of BTEC. All the communication syllabuses and parts of courses have been modified and rationalized in content and objectives. This rationalization has brought those involved in pre-vocational and the so-called academic communication work closer together in many respects. We do not subscribe to value judgements about the relative merit of, say, A-level Communication Studies and BTEC People in Organizations. It is a fact that pre-vocational courses do not require as much explicit knowledge and use of theory as their GCE and GCSE counterparts. But there is still much common ground, not least in terms of those basic principles which underlie any communication practice. The BTEC National skills statement (see p. 136) represents a set of objectives that A-level teachers could do well to take on board. Pre-vocational communication is not utilitarian *per se*; practical work is a worthy part of any communication course.

Our purpose

The main purpose of this book is to talk about what we teach and how we teach it. We will offer straight ideas about topics, concepts, and teaching methods. To this extent, this book takes a practical approach. We cannot please everyone, but we hope that every reader finds some ideas, and even some teaching methods or approaches, which they can take away and use. You will therefore gather that this book may do a little bit of preaching and flag-waving, but on the whole it will mark out territory and suggest possible routes across it. With the exception of some remarks in this chapter, we are not really interested in arguing the case for communication as a subject. If you are reading this book, then you are likely to be a practising communication teacher, or you think you will be one, or you are just curious. Whichever you are, we think it best to talk about the teaching. So this is not a book which espouses any particular educational theory. Nor will you find that this opening chapter is in any sense built on references to such theory or to the luminaries of that theoretical world.

The philosophy behind this book and communication work

On the other hand, we are very prepared to offer some kind of philosophy on communication teaching as we see it. This isn't a justification, it is simply an account of the way we see things. These ideas are woven into this book. You may find them useful to argue through if you need to build or rebuild a communication course.

To begin with, we take the view that one is dealing with a *process*, in the case of any example of communication. As a process, communication is something continuous and active, with no boundaries and no beginning or end. As communicators we are everything that we have been and that our culture has been. But this does not mean that all is chaos. What we do is to examine parts of the process, and see how they fit together. One looks at different theories for describing that process. And still one can deal in some principles – that communication will always have a purpose and a context, for example, and that such factors will always affect how communication takes place. So there are basics to deal with and to build on.

We also prefer to *integrate the semiotic approach* to communication with that of process. Communication is indeed all about the construction and use of signs and meaning, from one point of view. It is perfectly possible to see signification as working within process. Indeed, signs are the visible part of process. Unless one is able to make signs, to encode and decode them, then one lives in a meaningless world, unable to build bridges with others.

We accept that our communication techniques and sharing of meanings are rooted in often unacknowledged social, cultural, economic and political *experiences and traditions*. We all create our own meanings for and interpretations of communication acts in order to understand ourselves and the societies in which we live. Our readings of messages reflect our cultural and personal beliefs, biases and expectations. No two people will make an identical interpretation of the same text. They may make interpretations similar enough for them to agree about its meaning in general, or at least to agree as to why their interpretations differ. Since we are surrounded by messages from the various mass media it is essential that educational experience should enable people to analyse these messages and to understand how they are created. An understanding of the general processes of communication provides a way to probe the nature of media messages. At the heart of the study of communication is an attempt to understand and to make use of the processes and methods by which people use culturally-based signs and codes to express themselves and to share meanings with other people.

Another point which we would take as basic is that all study of communication is concerned with *how and why communication takes place*. We may study it for interest and pleasure; we may wish to understand it so that we can become better communicators. But it is still fundamental to be able to explain why we communicate as and when we do. It is also crucial to understand how we carry on this process if we are to understand other people and be understood by them.

We would also take the view that all communication courses can, in varying proportions, be described as being about *description, interpretation and practice*. That is to say, we must be able to describe accurately what is happening when communication takes place. We must then make sense of what we know. Finally, we must take something of our learning and put it into practice to become effective communicators.

This notion of becoming *an effective communicator* should also be implicit in even 'academic' courses. What is the use of knowledge and understanding if we can do nothing with it? And we do believe that it is possible to talk about effective communication, without invoking a rationale which is solely functional and instrumental. Being an effective communicator is obviously about communicating clearly what we mean, and being understood by others as a consequence. But it is also about personal qualities, such as consideration for others. An effective communicator takes into account as many factors in a given situation as possible. Being effective is not just about getting your own way, or delivering so many customers per minute to an advertising client. It is also about elements such as compassion and sympathy. An effective communicator will have the skill of empathy and will use it.

Another assumption which underlies our approach and which may underpin any communication course is that one is *teaching concepts which relate to skills*. These concepts are summarized in terms, factors, and models. They identify elements in the communication process, and help describe how communication is used and how it is carried on. They help both description and interpretation. From one point of view, when constructing a course, one must sort out what concepts are to be taught, explicitly or implicitly. But ideas are no good unless they inform practice.

In some quarters the notion of communication skills has become a dirty word because it has been misused, most frequently as a way of glossing over the fact that one may feel one is teaching something rather basic and very functional in a course which is in truth only generating job fodder. But in a more proper sense there is nothing wrong with teaching functional as opposed to intellectual or social skills.

If functional communication skills are approached as unproblematic, self-evident, mechanistic tricks which will make one a 'good' communicator, then this denies the subtle problem-solving choices that any communication task presents. Even in the simplest act of communication there are many choices to be made about what, why, when and how. For example, a model letter for a job application represents only a selection of topics and approaches: the writer of an actual letter must also make particular choices about vocabulary, information, structure, layout, tone and style, all of which reflect their personality, their view of who will read it and of the desired effect on this person. *Functional skills* presuppose a context of *intellectual and social skills*, of knowledge and under-standing. A communication course should deal with all three types of skill – all are valuable in terms of personal as well as vocational development.

This also leads on to the point that, even in overtly vocational communication courses or programmes, an effective course will still *develop the person and their capacity to handle relationships*, as well as *their ability to take effective action*. We take it as basic that a communication course should, in various degrees, be concerned with these three kinds of development.

In talking about functional and social skills or relationships and action in the same breath, we run the risk of being accused of trying to reduce what is complex and personal to a set of simplistic rules and doubtful nostrums for social success. At the same time, it is true that one can identify agreed skills, and identify some conventions of behaviour that are likely to contribute to successful outcomes of interaction in personal and social terms. Not only do we think that it is reasonable to deal in various communication skills, but also we think that *knowledge and awareness brings the power to control*. So the argument for teaching an understanding of what is happening when we communicate is that it gives those with that understanding the ability to use it to modify their communication behaviour. This does not mean that one has to use theory or abstract terms. One does not have to get deep into semiology to convey the idea that many communication problems stem from the fact that the relationship between signs and meanings is arbitrary and culturally conditioned.

We are also writing out of a belief that *communication cannot be neutral per se* – that all utterances have behind them a weight of cultural attitudes and values. Part of the point of at least some communication courses is to identify and articulate these assumptions, and to try to evaluate the relative degrees of selection and bias which have formed them.

Finally, we consider it a basic principle that, begging a few minor qualifications, *communicative competence is learned and not inherited*. It is our philosophy that learning about communication is learning about what we have learned, and how we have learned it. Again, this knowledge gives us the potential for re-learning how we communicate. People always have the capacity for change. But that capacity may not be used unless the individual sees a way of chang-ing and a reason for changing. Learning of any kind puts power in the mind of the learner. Communication practical work encourages use of that power to benefit the individual as a person, as a social being, and as a maker of communication in all its various forms.

5

Figure 1.1 Student-centred learning of communication

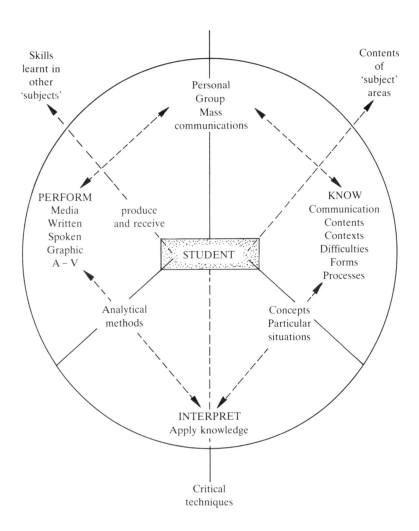

Some special features of communication work

Having dealt with the assumptions and philosophy underpinning our approach to communication work, we would now like to turn to our ideas about what is distinctive in communication study and practice. We are not claiming that all topics, concepts, or teaching approaches to communication are unique in themselves (though some are). But we do think that when you put these together, you have something different, valuable and interesting.

First, there is the holistic approach – that is to say, communication teachers are dealing in a body of theory which pulls together and deals with both face-to-face communication, and mass communication. Acts of and experiences of communication figure largely in our lives, so we think that it is distinctive and useful that there is such an approach which attempts to make coherent sense of these acts and experiences.

Then there is the question of the range of media dealt with, both in theory and in practical work. This is particularly relevant when one discusses the relationship of communication to English or to media studies. Clearly, the three (call them subjects if you like) do co-relate. But equally obvious is the fact that only the broad communication approach accommodates all media or languages. It is significant that English in particular has been the subject from which many communication teachers have come, and that it is the subject which has recently tried to accommodate media elements in particular within, for example, GCSE syllabuses. However, communication teaching has already become established as a separate discipline, so one must accept these subjects as being complementary, and not try to duplicate work which communication courses are already covering.

Another point which seems distinctive to communication work is the integration of theory and practice. One should inform the other; indeed, one can teach out of one or the other. One may draw conclusions about communication factors and principles from an activity which has been carried out, or one may explain concepts and then both reinforce them and make them 'real' through the experience of some activity.

Communication work is also distinctive in the support which it can offer to other subjects in the curriculum. Indeed, it may be unique in its central role within any curriculum. Some people even feel that there should not be such a separate subject or module on the timetable, but that all communication work should be taught in the context of other subjects. However, we think that this would not only ignore what is distinctive about communication theory, but also

7

that it would undermine the effective application of communication to other work. For example, it makes more sense to teach visual analysis, signification and meaning at one time, and then apply them to art, media, and geography, rather than duplicate effort. More importantly, it is unlikely that geography teachers would ever take such an approach, perhaps commenting on ways in which geography enshrines cultural attitudes and values in the apparently neutral pictures which are used to illustrate some textbooks.

Chapter two

What does one teach?

This is of course the question facing anyone in communication teaching at the beginning of a course. The existence of a syllabus is some help, but no real answer. It gives one terms of reference, but it isn't a course plan. Experience certainly helps, but it doesn't necessarily make the answer any easier. In fact it sometimes makes things more difficult because one has accumulated more material which one wants to use.

It is also a truism that content and method play off one another, so we are already having some problems in designing this chapter to deal with *what* one teaches, and leaving *how* one teaches until the next chapter! But that is also an inherent problem in teaching any communication course. What one gets across is as important as how one gets it across. So we are going to regard these two chapters as two ways of getting to the same place.

In a sense we are also putting our heads in the lion's den by incorporating BTEC National because it is largely supposed to be led on a skill basis, to be all about practice and method. However, first it is true that skills are present in any communication course, and are as much a part of context as anything else. Second, we shall demonstrate that the notion of skills extends beyond functional competence. Third, activities must in fact be concerned with ideas and principles – of communication in our case. And fourth, when for example one is dealing in negotiating skills or team/group skills, one is often drawn back into explaining the ideas which describe effective communication, and which help the student interpret what is going on. The same argument is true for GCSE, notwithstanding its practical inflexion. In other words principles and practice go hand-in-hand. The extent to which one or the other is made explicit on a course may depend on a number of things, including the needs and abilities of the particular students concerned. But to pretend that the two do not exist and have a co-relationship is nonsensical, and we do not propose to deal in nonsense.

What we are going to do in this chapter is to deal with basic elements of content such as skills, concepts, and communication formats. These are building blocks, and we are also going to look at some possible structures, for GCSE, A-level and BTEC National. Of course, you may be dealing with other courses, other syllabuses, short courses, custom-built courses, but we think that there is something for everyone in this. And it should be helpful even to old hands to have something that they can bounce ideas off, disagree with, and reshape to suit their own needs.

There are at least two important elements to setting up the material to answer the title question for this chapter. One is to keep in mind your main objectives; the other is to create a synthesis of ideas and activities to get you to those objectives. Regarding these objectives, we would define them as the intended outcomes of a course or part of a course. The various communication syllabuses also assume this definition. Such outcomes are seen mainly in terms of knowledge and of skills which make use of that knowledge (see Communication GCSE: the reference to describing, interpreting, practising). The measuring and grading of achievement of such objectives is another matter, also described in syllabus documents. The most difficult outcomes to measure are those relating to personal development and social skills. Whatever the difficulty, it remains a valid objective for the student that these elements should be enhanced through the experience of the course.

We also take it that another prerequisite for organizing a course based on a syllabus is to gut the syllabus, and build its parts into your course plan. Do the same thing with past examination papers. We are not going to do this for you, partly because the specimen course plans will do this by implication and partly because we also want to emphasize the point that all communication courses have, and should have, a great deal in common.

It is also important to bear in mind that even syllabus-led courses should not be inflexible. You may teach things which are not going to be examined, but which should be taught because you believe in their importance. You may have objectives which are not in a syllabus, or may be using a syllabus within the context of, say, CPVE, so that your course plan has to answer other objectives.

So it is also understood that the ideas contained within this book will be modified by you, the reader. There will be topics that you wish to give more weight to. There will be special needs that require you to put in another unit of work and try to compress what is left. All the same, we would argue that most of what we do cover, especially as represented through the course plans, is going to have to appear somewhere. This is why we have chosen three large areas of work which cover two levels of age and ability, and two kinds of inflexion, both practical, one more academic.

To sum up: in the first place, if you are trying to devise what to teach on a communication course, then make a list of what you want your students to understand and to be able to do by the end of the course. Then make lists under the headings that we are about to deal with: communication skills, formats of communication, concepts, categories, uses. Check the skills in particular against the sort of activities that you wish the group to experience (see the next chapter). Check that you have covered the objectives and content of the syllabus, if you are working to one. Then all you have to do is to integrate these lists into the structure of a workable course plan – of which more later.

Having spoken of checklists, it is perhaps consistent that the sections which follow have the brevity of lists. Where appropriate, we will refer to other texts for amplification, for three reasons. One is that this book is designed to be brief, and not to count the trees in every avenue. Another is that mere repetition of what is available elsewhere is a waste of everyone's time. The last reason is that we wish to avoid slipping into the slough of condescension.

One last point – and a tricky one. A question that we are often asked is what does one teach at a given level? The idea of 'level' is in itself a problem. The intellectual, personal and social development of individuals in groups, even in the school system, can vary widely. To some extent we have grasped this nettle in the course plans offered. We may also make cautious recommendations in the rest of the text. But in the end, unless some concept of activity is prescribed by a syllabus, it is a matter for the good judgement of the teacher as to what he or she includes in course content and method.

Communication skills

We take these to be to do with how one communicates effectively. Skills have much to do with performance, and may aid or impede communication. A student's skills may be rated in degrees. Skills are activities, cerebral or motor, which one may acquire with the general objective of improving communication with others. So a skill is something which the student learns from scratch, or which is enhanced. The development of skills through a communication course will help the student to think more effectively and to create communication more appropriately than they could before they started the course. Such communication, it should be emphasized, includes the ability to deal with other people sensitively.

What does one teach?

It is important to strike a balance between seeing skills as something merely mechanical (and without personal or social dimensions), and a view which makes acts of communication such a mysterious business that the idea of controlling verbal and non-verbal behaviour to good effect is felt to be impossible, and rather tasteless. A course which is only concerned with teaching students the conventions of a few formats of communication, which they then reproduce in an examination, is sterile. Equally it is dishonest to pretend that one cannot learn a few ground rules of performance which actually do enhance one's dealing with others, or one's chances of success in a job interview. The fact that there is no absolute formula for instant success in such matters is no excuse for not trying to improve our relationships and social performances.

We suggest that there are four general categories of communication skill: intellectual, functional, interpersonal, and group. Interpersonal skills are themselves defined through further sets: social, perceptual, presentational, and listening. There are overlaps between the sets and the categories, as is partly evident in the elaboration which now follows, and which offers you the first items of course content which you may want to put on your checklists.

Intellectual skills

Some of the most important activities that students can learn to perform happen in their heads. All communication starts and ends in the mind. Ironically, we do not have the space to intellectualize about the subject, but offer the following items from our experience. We should say, incidentally, that in no way are we claiming that these intellectual skills belong to communication study in particular.

It could be said that most of the intellectual activities that we wish to describe are to do with information – acquiring it, making sense of it, using it. We may be doing these things in many examples of communication activity, including social situations, so it is fair to regard practice of these particular intellectual skills as being most important. Thus one may talk about *selecting, comparing, ordering, prioritizing, categorizing, analysing, summarizing, problem-solving, and decision-making.*

These are skills which also come into perception. Many of them are skills which can be developed through any exercise in gathering, processing and representing information. The subject could be anything – preferences in popular music for instance – but the skills are there, probably in conjunction with the use of social skills if the pupil is conducting interviews, and with graphic skills if they are putting together results of their survey in such a form. There are

Figure 2.1 Model for communication skills – referring to perception – as shown by a student/pupil

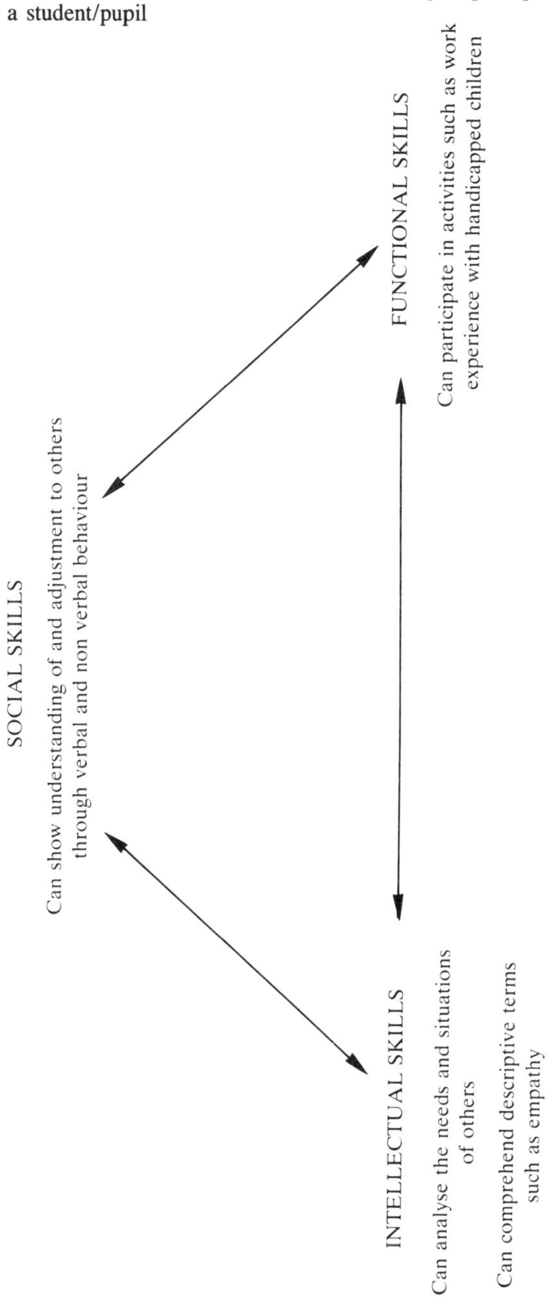

SOCIAL SKILLS

Can show understanding of and adjustment to others through verbal and non verbal behaviour

FUNCTIONAL SKILLS

Can participate in activities such as work experience with handicapped children

INTELLECTUAL SKILLS

Can analyse the needs and situations of others

Can comprehend descriptive terms such as empathy

also many situations in which and through which one might develop problem-solving and decision-making. In a more conscious sense, any kind of group work may be used to develop these skills.

Interpersonal – social skills

These are the life skills which enable us to get on with others. It is not necessary to enter into a long disquisition on any of the inter-personal skills which follow because they are described elsewhere, including our previous work (Burton, G. and Dimbleby, R. (1988) *Between Ourselves* London: Edward Arnold; Dimbleby R. and Burton, G. (1985) *More Than Words* London: Methuen). Enough will be said to make our meanings clear. Social skills include the ability to control non-verbal behaviour effectively; to offer recognition to others; to empathize; and to offer feedback in conversation.

Interpersonal – perceptual skills

These are the skills which we use when noticing verbal and non-verbal behaviour in others, in order to evaluate their attitudes, personality and emotional state. It is a skill to notice detail, as well as to avoid perceptual error when making sense of the information thus obtained. A conscious effort of intelligence is needed to make best use of the information obtained in perception, and then to communicate effectively.

Interpersonal – listening skills

These are well documented in other texts such as Nicki Stanton's *What Do You Mean, Communication?* (London: Pan, 1982). This refers to such activities as giving positive feedback to the speaker, asking check questions, and paying attention to what is said as much as how it is said.

Interpersonal – presentation skills

We use these when presenting ourselves to others (see also Goffman, E. (1959) *The Presentation of Self in Everyday Life*, Harmondsworth: Penguin). They are the kind of skills we want our students to acquire in order to put themselves across effectively when making formal oral presentations, when talking to members of the public, or to future employers. They are fundamentally about controlling verbal and non-verbal behaviour, in order to present an appropriate persona. They are about making ourselves attractive and likeable to others.

Group skills

The ability to become involved effectively in group activities, and to contribute well to groups, is a valuable one. Clearly, interpersonal skills are of relevance here. But it is also useful to put on our agenda of content what is called elsewhere task and maintenance role behaviour. The skills lie in being able to offer ideas; offering approval of others' ideas; evaluating others' ideas; summing up effectively, and so on. These are also skills which can be explained, practised, and drawn out of activity. They are especially valuable in the sense that traditional and conservative models of learning have emphasized individual achievement, and the pupil's separate learning relationship with the teacher (who is the essay for?!). But there is another tradition of activity and involvement with others, now given the seal of approval through GCSE, which demands that pupils should co-operate with others. So it follows that the practice of positive skills is in this respect valuable for the individual, and for the group, for learning how to cope after formal education.

Functional skills – general

By these we refer to the ability to produce communication in written or graphic formats (though a computer programme would also be another legitimate example). Thus writing a letter, designing a poster, or creating a pie chart would all be activities which require functional skills – the ability to handle standard conventions and to make the item required. Formats will be discussed further on pp. 21–3.

Functional skills – media technology

By these we refer to the ability to use the technologies associated with print, audio and visual production, albeit at a basic level and with amateur equipment. To make an audio recording of an interview involves functional skills, though no great expertise. Some teachers still have an unnecessary fear of using recorders, word processors, etc., a fear usually not shared by their pupils. Even at a simple level, hands-on experience and direct activities are valuable in themselves, and promote an understanding of professional mass-media activity. They can demystify the media.

There is a fundamental problem in that the education system is lamentably short of technological resources. While it is desirable to give pupils the experience of handling technology and of using it to understand media operations, still if you have few such resources, it need not devalue a communication course and should not be an objection to embarking on one. There are other kinds of practical work. Projects and their terms of reference may employ other media. Study of the mass media may have to depend more on examining products and source material in order to understand the process of production.

Having, we hope, reassured those in impoverished situations, we would like to go on to speak positively of the value of developing a degree of functional skill with media technology. It is an obvious fact of life that our everyday experience is laced richly with these technologies, for example either directly when we use a microcomputer or indirectly when we watch satellite-link broadcasts. Being able to use some technologically-based means of communication, both as receiver and producer, is a valuable part of developing our literacy in all forms of communication.

Our ancestors needed certain knowledge and skills to operate in an environment dominated by 'natural' things. Our environment naturally includes a wealth of technology and artifacts. We need appropriate knowledge and skills to operate successfully in this world of technology and to understand the mass media in particular. Education should reflect these needs. The very notion of education acknowledges that there must be conscious and structured activity which develops skills. There are many useful ideas and skills which have to be learnt within the institution of education because there is no reason to suppose that they will be learned in any other way. Concepts within terms such as 'audience', 'information source', 'economic and political control', 'genres', 'decoding messages', cannot be left to be picked up in the home or on the street. Teaching is founded on the idea that it is valuable to develop consciousness of ideas and of ways of using these.

It is reasonable to argue that we owe it to young people to provide them with the analytical tools for reading the media messages which bombard them. At the same time we should try to equip them to express themselves through the various media technologies. Today it is in a sense part of literacy to be able to use a camera, a telephone, an audio tape recorder or a word processor. In a 'human communication' (as opposed to a 'technical communication') course our aim would be to enable people to use communication technologies, but not necessarily to know how the machines actually work.

Such technological literacy must also be rooted in socio-economic understanding. Mass media and information technology systems are also social institutions, and to understand them calls for a study of social relationships. Such is the comprehensiveness of the study of communication that it can provide perspectives which bring together theory and practice, functional and social elements. Readers will find that the issues of media studies in particular have been well addressed elsewhere, for example by Masterman (1986), Alvarado (1987), and by Lusted (1989): for further details of these books see pp. 143–5.

Categories of communication

Pace the A level in Communication Studies, there are five categories of communication that one may cover in a course. These are: 1, intrapersonal; 2, interpersonal; 3, group; 4, mass; 5, extrapersonal. Under these headings fall a range of subsidiary topics described in the A-level syllabus, and to some extent, the GCSE syllabus. They also appear *de facto* in many other communication courses. These are broad brushstrokes on the canvas, but it is still worth deciding whether to make them or not when planning to teach communication. Our own view is that one cannot teach any communication course for a year or more without addressing some of 2, 3, and 4, and a little bit of 1. How one deals with the relevant topics and concepts is of course another matter.

It is understood that in the A level one can be more explicit about concepts, and cover all the categories (though extrapersonal communication is still regarded as being a little bit esoteric, even so – see p. 19 below). Nevertheless, as we have said, even on a vocational course, the concepts must be lurking close behind the activities. The teacher at least needs to know what they are, if only to have a proper rationale for a course. It is no good carrying out activities in an intellectual vacuum. Even at the sixteen-plus level (GCSE or RSA Communication in Business level 2), one needs to explain some basic principles of communication such as the notion of audience. And many students in such classes are capable of comprehending the use of terms such as perception or feedback. We do not mean to be condescending when we say that the trick is to relate the ideas to real experience, to the vocational needs of the students in each case. More will be said about key concepts later in this chapter. However, to make the point about concepts and topics in relation to categories, the following elaboration may be useful.

The remarks which follow are based on an assumption of basic competence in a 16-year-old. Again, we would emphasize that, even with confidence in the ability of these students to deal in ideas, it is not always necessary to use the communication language up front. It will be sufficient if the ideas and their relevance are evident through implication and application. Equally, one has to remember that the GCSE, for example, does assume that pupils can so describe and interpret.

Figure 2.2 Model relating categories, forms, and uses of communication

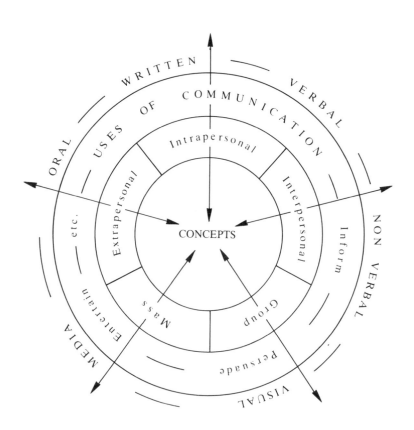

Intrapersonal communication is concerned with the needs which motivate us, and the way in which we communicate according to the notions of self which we have in our heads. How we see ourselves affects how we communicate.

Interpersonal communication would have an agenda which includes something about perception, about the use of non-verbal behaviour, and about the ways that we present ourselves.

Group communication would deal in constructive and obstructive behaviour in groups, with role and its effect on groups, with informal and formal group experience (such as meetings).

Mass communication would essentially deal with the media. In practice, we prefer to deal with the press and with television, because this spans a range of written and visual experience. One would wish to look at where the messages come from, how they are put together, where they are going to, and how they may affect the audience. Specifically, one is likely to deal with notions such as genre, convention, construction and representation. One is therefore also likely to look at the quality and the popular press, at modes of television such as news, documentary and soaps. It is also likely that one would link with this category some work on the applications and social implications of new technology.

Extrapersonal communication comprises communication directly with anything other than another person. In practice, this category would include specialized topics such as artificial intelligence (and communication with machines), or communication with other creatures (such as the famous study of Washoe the chimp, who was taught to use a limited vocabulary of sign language). The very specialization of such topics means that in practice this category is rarely taken on by teachers even of A level as a distinct course unit. Examples such as the above may be used successfully to raise and to illustrate issues concerning the production of signs and meaning, or the nature of decoding and meaning.

This thumbnail sketch elaborating the idea of categories and fleshing out the content, necessarily brings up the question of which formats of communication (activities) one also undertakes. (More of these later in this chapter.) Some vocational syllabuses lead on such formats. Their objectives are generally ones that the student should be able to perform. But again this begs the question of why they should learn to create given formats and be able to use them, and also the question of measuring such performances.

Behind all this, and not belonging to a specific category, lie general communication concepts and principles. These would, for example, be that all communication is a process of which messages and meanings are a part; that all communication is bound by unwritten rules or conventions; that being an effective communicator is about making sense of what we receive as well as being able to control what we say and do; and that many of the most significant messages that we deal in are concerned with values and beliefs about ourselves, about others, about the way we live.

Uses of communication

These elements of content may be dealt with very simply. What we are suggesting is that any course should have a built-in check to ensure that it has addressed itself to the basic purposes that we have in using various forms of communication. This is particularly relevant to questions of message treatment, and for notions of style in written communication. A statement of use or purpose also pins down terms of reference when evaluating the effectiveness of the communication that the student has created. If they have committed themselves to creating posters and leaflets in order to persuade local people to join a club that they themselves belong to, then that student must demonstrate that they can use persuasive devices.

Broadly speaking, we can distinguish between *social* or *functional* purposes in using communication. That is to say, we are trying to develop or modify our social relationships with others in some way, or we are trying to give or obtain information. However, in practice these two apparently separate purposes are inextricably linked. Authors writing a book are seeking to provide information, but they are also inevitably creating a relationship with the reader. A stranger seeking directions from a local person is seeking to obtain information, but he or she is also inevitably making human contact with another person.

Clearly this section has relevance to the kind of tasks that one is likely to set, as well as to the forms of communication chosen in order to achieve the purposes for a given audience. In this sense, there is value in focussing the pupils's attention on principles of communication – indeed in teaching these by stealth. Examples of use would be: to inform, to warn, to persuade, to encourage, to apologize, to explain, to entertain.

As a coda to this section it is worth pointing out that some pupils find it securing to be able to categorize communication in various ways. These people would find it encouraging to realize that most, if not all of their communicative experience can be organized under the various headings of categories, uses and forms. So at this point it seems appropriate to move on to forms and formats.

Forms and formats

Bedevilled as we are by a potential span of study that is today the world as we know it, and tomorrow the meaning of life, one of the problems for teachers of communication is to tie down what specific parts of experience are proper areas of study for their group. In particular it is necessary to decide which examples of communication one wishes the students to experience and become skilled in. Some syllabuses partly solve this problem by being format-led, and specifying what the pupil must be able to do by the end of a course. Some create problems (GCE and GCSE) by requiring performance under examination conditions, but not specifying which formats must be understood until the candidate faces the examination paper. Again, those that specify formats may seem to be limiting, and the teacher may wish to provide a wider experience. And a number of syllabuses require a piece of communication to be created as assessed course work (usually called a project).

In fact, in terms of examination conditions, there are actually a limited number of written and graphic formats which may reasonably be demanded. It is also the case that up to a point, the ability to perform in one format will provide competence in comparable examples. For instance, if a pupil can design the cover of a booklet, then they can also use the same skills and criteria to create and judge their own poster design. Yet another parameter for pinning down this kind of course content is the criteria of what will be useful to the student in future work and social experience. In some respects this may lead one into teaching some specialized formats. For example, it is important for business students to be able to handle a report format, whereas one cannot argue for this being a priority in GCSE. There is a kind of irony in the fact that the still ubiquitous essay format is actually the least useful kind of communication for any student. It does have value in respect of structuring thought and argument, and in respect of creating objective style. Even so, we would suggest that an effective communication essay should include topic headings, lists of points where necessary, diagrams or models where appropriate – indeed, anything which helps make its meaning clear, regardless of any traditional aesthetics of style (which have their origins in a largely defunct tradition of rhetoric).

So what now follows are lists of formats – that is, specific examples that fall within general forms of communication. You will notice that the various written and visual formats may (like the oral tasks) also be pulled into your course-planning under the heading of method, as examples of activities which can (and often should) be incorporated within a course. In providing these bare lists we are not proposing a teaching method which sets them as tasks in isolation. Ideally, they should appear as something which is dealt with either through a case study or through some longer and more authentic activity. For example, letter-writing might be practised in role within the terms of an invented but plausible situation which the teacher has created. Or a checklist might appear as part of an actual activity in which a group of pupils are, for example, organizing and supervising a trip of some kind for local primary school children.

One final point – examples of communication do not simply divide into written and visual for our convenience. The value of creating leaflets or wall charts, for example, is precisely that they combine words with visuals.

Written formats

Letters; articles; questionnaires; checklists; fact sheets; memoranda; dialogue; short reports; scripts.

Visual – general

Leaflets; booklets; posters; wallcharts; many advertisements.

Visual – graphic

Flow charts (algorithms); schedules; graphs; pie charts; bar charts; pictograms; ground plans; grids; logos.

Visual – pictorial

Storyboards; see also aspects of those under general, above.

Oral formats

Formal presentations; informal talks to a group; interviews; conversation; group discussion.

Media formats

Newspaper page layouts; audio tape of an interview; video tape of group work; publicity tape slide; magazine layout.

With regard to the placing and the sequence of activities for such formats within a course, there are one or two things to bear in mind. One is that it is useful to introduce visual activities near the beginning of a course in order to assert the range of possible activities. It is also useful to consider that even able students may be surprisingly incompetent at design tasks because, compared with writing, they have not had much experience of these. In general, it is a good idea to develop from informal to formal writing, from interpersonal to group activities, from the general visual formats to the specific graphic examples, throughout the course. But otherwise, the general principles of layout or of formats having conventions, are universal and do not predicate any particular sequence.

At the end of this section we wish to make a couple of qualifications and a reference to information technology. First, we are aware that some teachers are hard-pressed for time and may regard the prospect of incorporating all the above in, for example, a one-year course with some trepidation. In fact, we would argue that it could be done. But it is also the case that it is not the end of the world if one has to be a little selective. Second, we are aware that some people would wish to see examples of information technology included. To this we would say two things. One is, fine if you have the machines and the competence, but for reasons presented already one cannot make it a *sine qua non* of a communication course that there should be use of (most obviously) micro computers. The other point is that, without wishing to split semantic hairs, such examples are not so much formats as technological tools. It is nice to be able to produce a pie chart via a programme for a BBC micro, but it is still a pie chart for all that. Similarly, processed text in fact emerges from a communication tool which is just an improvement on the ball-point pen – though some improvement!

Terms or concepts

At this point in the chapter we are entering a thorny thicket, but, nothing daunted, propose clearing a way through. The issue of what concepts to teach is one that may provoke fierce argument. On the other hand, it is a fact that people are making such choices, and they are also made through examination papers. So without wishing to rely on a finite list of ideas, it should make sense to set up a further agenda which we hope represents pretty much what all experienced teachers of communication would wish to deal with.

Readers should remember that we are addressing them as teachers, and do not necessarily propose that every phrase or term used here can or should be used as given. The writers' experience is, naturally, that less able pupils have to be taught not only through the strategies described in the next chapter, but also in a more idiomatic language than we now choose to use. It is also the case that one has to conceive of at least two levels of comprehension, symbolized by GCSE and A-level. You, the teacher, will have to decide what your pupils or students can best take on. We are not attempting to replicate the kind of thorough definitions which occupy whole books in themselves (titles like O'Sullivan *et al.* (1983) *Key Concepts in Communication* London: Methuen, and Watson and Hill (1989) *A Dictionary of Communication and Media Studies* London: Edward Arnold). Also, we have ourselves written two other books which explain the concepts which follow in other terms (and through a glossary), for students and in more detail in the case of inter-personal communication. So we are trying to provide something more like a checklist of the more basic ideas, and would advise you to look at those other works for supplements to this chapter. In this book, compared with the others, the crucial difference is that under each item we are not trying to explain its meaning directly, so much as to make blunt statements about what we believe are the essentials that need to be put across to the pupil.

In making these points one thing that we are trying to do is to allay the anxieties of many teachers who have said to us, of GCSE and A level in particular, how does one know what ideas to teach? What is one meant to say about them? What are the essentials? These pages lay us open to criticism from those who wish to preserve the openness and the free growth of the subject. We don't think that we are impeding this, and we do think that it is time that this kind of agenda was set up – precisely to help the subject grow on some agreed basis.

It is worth reiterating that these concepts are not unique to the levels of GC(S)E. We have already argued that there may be good reasons in some cases for bringing in terminology for able voca-tional students, because the ideas must be there informing the prac-tice. One should not condescend to any of one's students, any more than one should use a register which is beyond them. It is all a matter of horses for courses, and never mind the syllabus. More particularly, the brief comments made with reference to each term should be helpful to anyone who wants to make ideas accessible to vocational students of modest ability, without actually using intimidating language. By way of example, the RSA Communication in Business level 3 syllabus makes explicit demands in respect of understanding terms and using communication models. Levels 1 and 2 do not. But there is no reason why students at levels 1 and 2 should not be prepared for the relative abstraction of level 3 through colloquial explanations and common-sense applications.

There is no need to create a mystique around theory in any discipline. In the case of GCSE one should be prepared to use some basic terms as well as the colloquial approach, not only for the same reasons but also because at least some of those pupils will want to go on to A level. So what follows is a list of communication concepts accompanied by a comment on the essential ideas that one would wish to get across to the pupils. We leave this to stand by itself as a statement of possible content.

Concepts and issues

First it can be said that the words *concept/terms/factors* are used interchangeably when talking about communication theory. That is to say, one is simply using a key word that identifies one part of the communication process. These terms or factors will also appear in communication models, which are graphic devices for relating the terms and for illustrating parts or the whole of the process. These factors may also be incorporated within statements of principle – apparent truths about the communication process, referring to how and why it takes place.

The word *element* is something more of a catch-all label, used to refer to items within a piece of communication which contribute to it. Thus, in the case of a badge, colour, shape, typeface, type size, wording, and graphics, may all be communication elements which contribute to the whole communication which is the badge. They contribute to its meaning. For a fuller discussion of communication processes and models we refer you to Dimbleby and Burton (1985) *More Than Words: an introduction to communication*, London: Methuen.

It will also be seen that the concepts listed below are organized in groups, mainly based on categories of communication. In particular, the concepts of the first group will relate to all the others, and it will be realized that those which are part of inter-personal communication are also relevant to the study of groups.

General terms

Process

The idea that communication is something continuous, that it flows like blood around the arteries, or channels of communication, of our working and social lives. It is worth using models to try and visualize this flow. Also make it clear that there are parts of the process, such as audience/receiver, which we examine separately. It is important to describe process in terms of specific examples, showing that, for instance, the creation and reading of a magazine advertisement is as much an example of process as is a conversation.

Uses

The idea that communication is used in different ways at different times for different reasons – informing, warning, persuading. It is important to get across the idea that all forms of communication can be used in different ways. Various types of television programme fit all kinds of uses. Equally, persuasion is not unique to advertising, for instance. It is valuable to make it clear that we use conversation in everyday life to carry out some strong persuasion.

Effective/appropriate

The idea that we can define when communication is being conducted in the 'right' way, and when it is having 'positive' effects. Basically, this is the case when the communicator has taken into account the communication factors listed below, especially the needs of the receiver of the communication, and the conventions of how that form of communication should be used. Since the notion of effectiveness includes factors within the process, such as recognizing the importance of who is the receiver of a piece of communication and what their needs are, then it makes sense to inculcate these terms as a kind of checklist. A good communication student never creates a piece of communication without using such a check, such terms of reference. (This is not to suggest that one creates a formula for unbridled success – merely that we can make it more probable than not that it will have some success. Nor is it to ignore important critical issues surrounding conventions and ideology which, nevertheless, one would suggest are best raised only with able pupils.)

Source/sender

The idea that all communication must start somewhere and that the individual or organization that it starts from influences the way the communication is expressed.

Receiver/audience

The idea that all communication goes somewhere, that the sender's view of what the audience is like will affect how they frame their communication, but that the receiver will also tend to take their own meanings from the communication, regardless of what was intended in the first place. Just as students on a course should have to work in a variety of formats, so also they should have to deal with a variety of audiences so that the effect of audience on what is said and how will be reinforced.

Purpose

All communication is put together with some purpose in mind, whether or not the sender is fully aware of what this is. Again, one can interpret the communication and its effects better if one is fully aware of what the real purpose of it is. It should become apparent that what we *think* someone's purpose is, is more important than what it *actually* is. The pupils will come to understand that we act on assumptions when decoding messages.

Context

The physical or social situation in which the communication takes place will always affect how it is understood, and will probably affect how it is put together in the first place. In terms of inter-personal and group communication, it is at least useful to discuss or simulate examples which may be described as public or private situations in order to get across the force of this concept. Try getting a pupil to role-play behaviour in public that they would normally use at home, and the point will have been made.

Channel/form

All communication has to be put into some form such as speech or pictures. Different forms have different qualities, and different advantages and disadvantages. The form used affects how the communication is put together and understood. Effective communicators weigh up the advantages of the various forms of communication available to them. It is often the case that we use more than one form of communication at a time. The number of forms that may be used through the medium of television in an evening news broadcast is a case in point. Students should be allowed to make decisions about the use of forms of communication during their course. They should practise the conventions of the form or format. On a more sophisticated level they should grasp the idea that the medium is indeed the message, and that the same message is transformed in various ways once cast in a form other than its original.

Medium/media

The term *medium* is often used in a generalized way to describe a means of communication. Strictly speaking, it should be applied to those examples which include more than one form, such as television. In this case, the viewer may be decoding simultaneously forms such as oral, written, non-verbal and visual, all of which are heard and seen. To this extent, the use of the term is to draw attention to the co-existence of various communication codes. It is also important to undercut any notion that one form simply dominates in a medium. It is often misleading to go along with simple statements such as 'television is a visual medium'. The term 'media' is used in two ways. In the first place it is well understood within the phrase 'mass media'. It is also the case that one may talk about 'media of communication', referring to the technology used to enable communication to take place.

Message

The message is what the sender means to say and what the receiver thinks they have said. The gap between these two can create a communication problem. Messages often work on two levels – what the sender intends to say, and what they say unintentionally (perhaps through non-verbal signs). It is important to get across the idea that we are often superficial in our reading of messages, in respect of interpersonal communications as well as through the mass media. It takes an effort to make a full interpretation of a piece of communication. Message content is about what is said, message treatment is about how it is said – the one complements the other.

Feedback

This is the response one gets from sending a message and the adjustment made because of that response. Giving and noticing feedback is a basic skill which helps, for instance, social interaction and listening. Pupils should understand that feedback is an integral part of perception in particular, where any interaction is a process of continual checking and adjustment to the other person. Exercises in which those involved try to cut off feedback – playing poker face, facing away from one another – soon make the point about the amount of feedback and message exchanging that goes on alongside bare words. Through such activities it should be understood that feedback may be negative, and not conducive to developing trust and effective communication between people.

Encoding/decoding

This is putting together and taking apart the message in its given form or medium – speaking and listening. The important thing is that if we do this carefully then we are more likely to understand and be understood. *Pace* comments on process made above, this kind of terminology becomes less formidable when one points out that talking and listening are everyday examples.

Conventions

These are the unwritten rules that govern how we use forms of communication. Life is full of conventions about how we talk in certain situations with certain people, as well as how we should lay out and use written formats, for example. Understanding and using these rules (not slavishly or uncritically) will make us more effective communicators. It will also help us understand how communication takes place. Rule-breaking exercises are essential for bringing home the point that the rules do exist. Examples of rudeness are usually examples of rule breaking. Young people greeting one another often provide interesting examples of people who have yet to learn conventions. But of course it is equally important to expose media conventions. A role-reversal exercise based on young women's magazines might make the point. And one can have fun with rule breaking the characters and plots of any one of television's current soap serials.

Signs

Try to get across the idea that all forms of communication that we use are made up of signs, and together these make up the message in communication. Signs are like words, gestures, or the use of focus in photographs. They tell us how to understand that communication. Pupils need to be able to identify signs in order to be able to work out what true meanings are in a piece of communication. Often these meanings add up to hidden messages. It is useful to get across the idea that signs are arbitrary, perhaps by playing with invented ones for everyday objects, perhaps by looking at hieroglyphs and characters from other languages.

Codes

It is in fact then difficult to avoid saying something about codes – sets of signs organized by rules (conventions). Again, it is not that hard an idea to get across. Most young people have sent 'secret' messages in class at some time. If you want a sophisticated example of code invention then try Tolkein's *Elvish*, described in detail at the end of (1965) *The Lord of the Rings* (Cambridge). And the point about signs being associated by rule, often in sequence, is well made if one tries to deal with a jumbled sentence, or asks pupils to try greeting someone without smiling.

Meaning

Meaning is what you think it is! At this level it is enough to equate the meaning with the message. The main thing to get across is first the idea of hidden meanings/messages, and second the idea that meanings are attached to signs because of conventions, not because

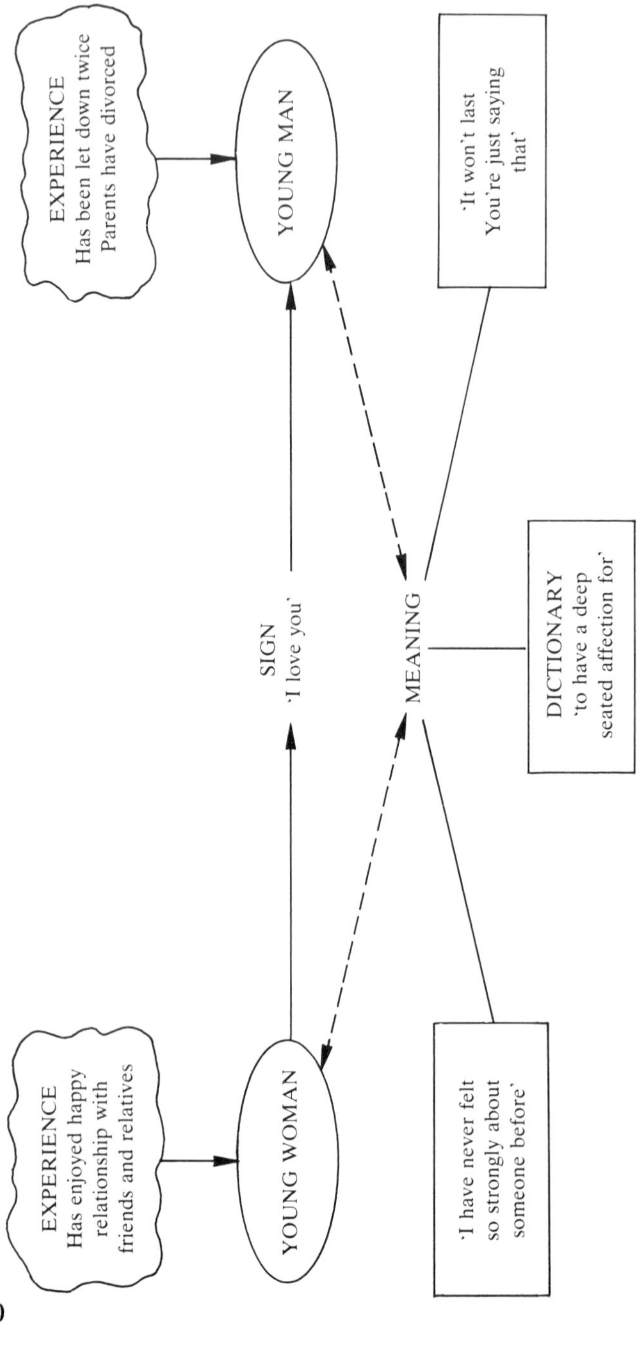

Figure 2.3 Model to illustrate the problem of sharing meanings

of some law of nature. So people disagree about meanings – another way of getting into communication problems. Ask students if they have heard phrases recently such as *that's not what I said* or *you obviously weren't listening* and you probably have an example of confused meaning and a breakdown of communication. They will also probably be interested in an investigation of meaning in pictures. You will make your own judgement as to whether or not you could use depictions of women by Velázquez and the photographers of *haute couture* magazines like Harper's in order to discuss why they are thought to have different meanings. Indeed, this kind of material ranges across a number of important communication terms and topics, not least of which is the point that meaning is culturally determined and is not absolute. The fact that meaning is relative to socialization within a given culture or subculture may be brought out in a number of ways. For example, one might look at the use of patois in Caribbean subcultures, or at the various meanings of non-verbal gestures across European nationalities.

Text

Refers to the material which we study, and is used in the broadest sense. So a text is any piece of communication in any form or medium, which we may analyse in terms of its signs and its structure in order to determine the meanings within the text, as well as how they are embedded in that text. A magazine advertisement or a situation comedy is a text, as much as is a newspaper article.

Intrapersonal communication

Self

Get across the idea that there is a difference between the way we see ourselves and the way that others see us, that we have ideal images of ourselves. What we think we are, what we believe others think we are, will affect our style or manner of communication, and may make it more or less effective.

Self-esteem

This is about how well we think of ourselves. Try to convey the idea that how well we think of ourselves affects how well we communicate with others; also the idea that everyone has things that they are good at and can feel good about.

Needs

These are the forces which drive us from within – they are the motivation for communication. A good communicator is honest about needs/motivation, and is good at weighing up the needs of others so that these can be taken into consideration when deciding how to communicate. If we think about real needs, then we are finding out why communication takes place. This concept has relevance across the range of categories: why might someone make 'unkind' remarks to another?; why do some people 'work harder' than others?; why do some people enjoy watching situation comedies on television?; why do people like us want to write a book like this one?!

Interpersonal communication

Perception

The art of weighing up other people and acting on judgements made. Perception is an integral part of communication between people. The main ideas to get across are as follows: that perception has two main parts – observation and making judgements; that we judge ourselves as well as others; that we need to perceive before we can decide on how we will start or continue communication with another person; that in particular, we perceive attitudes, emotions and personality in others; that the judgements we make in perceiving are greatly affected by our existing beliefs and values – we tend to want to confirm these beliefs and values.

As is often the case, exercises designed to expose what happens when communication goes wrong, or when rules are broken, are most revealing for most pupils. So anything designed to expose the false assumptions that we may make about elements such as age, occupation, and attributes, is useful: often magazine material helps here, though photographs of people known to the teacher can have even more impact. It is also important to deal with perception in 'live' situations, to make the point that we can modify our judgements, and improve our perceptual skills.

Non-verbal behaviour

This one is more a descriptive term than a concept, but it is still an important element in teaching interpersonal communication because NVB works on an emotional level, and is what we spend a lot of time perceiving. In this case, deal with a taxonomy of types of non-verbal behaviour to give it structure. You can find useful taxonomies in Michael Argyle (1983) *The Psychology of Interpersonal Behaviour* Harmondsworth: Penguin, and also in his (1987) *Bodily Communication* London: Methuen, additionally Dimbleby and Burton (1985)

More Than Words, and G.E. Myers and M.T. Myers (1986) *The Dynamics of Human Communication* New York: McGraw-Hill, provide accessible lists. But also deal with its effect in practice, especially, for example, the way that non-verbal cues are used to regulate conversation (e.g. turn-taking).

In terms of examining it and practising, put it into useful situations such as the job interview. In this case, it may be effectively related to perception, and to the problem of initial impression formation. Using observers and/or videotape, one can identify those non-verbal signs which carry meanings about personality, attitude, and emotional state.

Strategy

Those little packages of communication behaviour used for particular effects. Again, the idea is to illustrate these in a wide range of situations – for example, strategies for making excuses/appeasing others. Role plays can be an amusing way of bringing out the verbal and non-verbal behaviour that pupils use themselves. They can also observe strategies used, for example, by chat-show hosts who want to shut a guest up or wind up a programme.

Self-presentation

Is all about the kind of self we wish to put forward in a given situation. This may be called the *persona*, and the act we put on in presenting it may be called the performance. If your students comment that this is close to the idea of strategy, then give them a team point for being right. Get across the idea that we put on performances so that other people will achieve a certain view of us (usually favourable). Look at social performances when, for example, we will put on a show to make a complaint about something, or at professional performances when people will put on a show in order to maintain their job image, for example the doctor's bedside manner.

Barriers to communication

Again more of a topic than a concept, but it is important to deal with reasons why communication breaks down and misunderstandings occur. Discuss the different types of barrier, and most of all, get across through a variety of examples the idea that most barriers are in our heads. It is people's beliefs and attitudes which usually cause them to disagree, not to listen, and to misunderstand. This is also true when one is dealing with examples of racial prejudice or religious difference. It is useful to pinpoint the particular words or non-verbal signs that cause the problem, and to make the point that

33

it really is all about communication. Once more, video can be very helpful in this respect.

The fact that this segment can also be related to perception (or, rather, to poor perception) makes the point that one does need to keep on emphasizing the relationship between one concept and another, especially when lessons come days apart, and the pupils need to pick up the threads again. Straightforward lists and models on the board which provide a check and a plan of connections between one idea and another are very useful, depending on how concept-led your course is. It is worth remembering that, whatever the pleasures of active learning and practical work, pupils will not see underlying points unless you make them clear. Indeed, the danger of a largely activity-led approach is that pupils may enjoy it for its own sake, but not be able to make full use of the experience because it is not in a framework. It can be very reassuring to the less able, in particular, to have notes consisting of summary key statements. So-called theory does not have to be cast in a register outside their capacities simply because it is theory. Equally, it is dangerous to condescend to apparently lower-ability groups by assuming that anything resembling an abstraction is beyond their capacity to understand. Without wishing to be too glib about our task as teachers, it is often the case that we simply have to find our own strategies to put over the message.

Group communication (including organizations)

Role

The idea that one takes on a certain position with relation to other group members and that one communicates in a particular way. Roles usually have labels like 'leader' and 'joker'. The main point to convey is that certain roles have certain kinds of communication attached to them. Others will expect the role holder to talk in a certain way: the role holder will expect to talk in that way. One can move on to see what effects all this has on how group members get on with one another, and on how well they can make decisions. With more able students, one can present the idea that role has more than one meaning, and that, for example, one can talk about maintenance and task roles, as opposed to self-oriented roles. However, even if this is felt to be too difficult, at least one can put across the idea that some people in groups help the group as a whole to get along and get the job done, while others are self-absorbed and disrupt proceedings. This is what constructive and obstructive group behaviours are about. Through simulations, students can grasp the message that certain kinds of talk are helpful to discussions and the achievement of tasks, while others are not.

Goal

All groups have something that they are aiming for, whether it is to achieve a sense of belonging or to get a job done. The central message is that so long as group members are clear about their goal(s) and agree on them, then all goes well – otherwise there will be bickering and breakdown.

Co-operation

The word speaks for itself – but it is important that pupils understand that groups are about working together, and that they should have this experience themselves. With reference to concepts already mentioned, they can understand through observation and practice that behaving constructively and offering positive feedback helps other group members understand what they mean, as well as simply to get on better with them.

Identity

The idea that groups and their members have particular identities marked out by their communication behaviour, whether it be speech-style or clothes. Pupils need to understand what examples of such identity there are around, what the communication actually stands for, and that this identity is often important for people joining groups to achieve a sense of security and self-image that they do not have as individuals.

It is most obvious to look at social groups, family groups and work groups, but it may well be that most mileage will be obtained from examination of subcultural groups. Your students will very possibly include members of these, or be very sensitive to nuances of dress, hair-style, and speech that mark out such groups. The problem is to go beyond description to significance. As is the case with the allied case of stereotyping, it is easy to describe appearance and behaviour, not so easy to lead on to the significance of these in terms of why they happen, and what they may stand for. Teachers will use their own judgement as to whether it is better with such topics to look introspectively at the pupils' own experience, or better to use examples which are a little distant from this because they can be treated more objectively.

Norms

The idea that the group has beliefs and values – ones which the individual members don't necessarily hold. In this case the main things to get across are what examples of norms there are around, and how these can influence group behaviour. One could look at examples of where people will do things in groups that they would not wish to or dare to on their own – football hooligans, for instance. One can also look at reasons why individuals are pressured out of groups (because they are not conforming).

Small group networks

Whether one is talking about social groups or work groups, it is useful to look at various models which illustrate the frequency and direction of flow of communication in small groups. The main points to bear in mind are that this way one can weigh up contributions, bondings, and some group roles in a relatively objective manner. It sounds formidable to be talking about a sociometric model, but when pupils are dealing with people whom they know and talking about who is close to whom, or who is a social leader and why, then the drawings make sense. For examples of how such sociometric models can be simply developed, we refer you to our previous books, *More Than Words* (1985) (chapter 3), and *Between Ourselves* (1988) (chapter 6).

Large group networks

In this case, one is concerned to explain how and why communication does or does not flow in a company or institution. The idea of a network can be described in terms of the links in a communication chain which are organized so as to process information in an organization.

One may describe this, but also convey the point that being able to map out lines of communication helps show up where there are weak links in the chain. In a general sense a network model may describe the relationship between the various departments of an organization. Models can also say something about the ethos of an organization. Ask your students to draw a model for their school/college and they will likely base it on groups of workers, with the principal or head at the top of the paper. This betrays our socialization. Ask them to redraw the model with the word students/pupils in a circle in the middle of the paper, and then carry on. The resulting diagram usually emerges as molecular rather than hierarchical, and thus shows the sense of the student's central value in an educational organization.

Organization problems

There are usually three – failures of means of communication, badly organized networks and people problems. People problems are often to do with poor motivation and unhelpful attitudes. Again, try to bring out the idea that not only does a company not work efficiently if there are such problems, but also that the large group which is the workforce will not be happy. Previous work on barriers to communication is especially relevant here.

If this topic is tackled by non-business students, then it is worth remembering that not only is your own school or college a rich source of material, but also that a number of them will have part-time jobs or belong to clubs.

Motivation

Re-examine the idea of needs, but in a work context. Industrial psychologists would shudder at this simplification. But it is true that most people are motivated when their needs are recognized and rewarded. The problem is that these needs may change. Some kind of work-based simulation here would bring out the fact that people are not necessarily motivated by cash, but also, for instance, by variations in routine and by being given responsibility. Try it on those whom you are teaching!

Conflict

Get across the idea that conflict in work groups occurs because of conflicting needs (perhaps two people want to be leader of the group). Conflict can also be dealt with effectively by practising a meeting simulation, through which one can examine where conflict comes from and how it may be allayed. The conventions of formal meetings are intended to reduce conflict anyway, but one can also point out how certain kinds of communication behaviour (giving strokes to others) will reduce the likelihood of conflict.

Decision-making

Get across the idea that groups in organizations are usually brought together to make decisions, and that groups often make decisions better than individuals. Practice in brain-storming and problem-solving through some practical activity usually puts this over. For an example of a simple brain-storming exercise, see p. 88 in the section on things to do with magazines.

Here one can also refer back to small group networks and models, describing how some groups are better at making decisions than others because they are organized and operated in a certain way. Though this will not be a priority topic for some teachers, you may still want to use it in the sense that any communication student is going to undertake group activities at some point in their course. If they learn how to organize themselves in order to complete tasks effectively and happily, then there is no harm in that.

What does one teach?

Mass communication

Mass

One needs to sort out what the term 'mass' means if one is going to look at the mass media and how they communicate. So in this case one needs to get over the idea that it is about scale – large-scale production, large-scale distribution of messages, large audiences, and large amounts of profit. Mass communication is essentially about the creation of messages by the few for the many.

This sense of scale also applies to costs and investments. Those who are prepared to invest a great deal of money in such means of communication and in manufacturing messages will have an effect. Often that effect is to give pleasure and bring profit. Thus one is led into a rationale for an examination of the media, of audience and of possible effects on that audience.

Visual analysis – image-reading

This is really about a process rather than a concept, but because so much media material is visual, it is important to get pupils to decode pictures in a methodical way – to get at the meaning of the communication. The methods are adequately described in other texts, but essentially it is about looking at the detailed content, treatment and then meanings of, for example, magazine pictures. One can look at what the camera is doing, at details of colour, lighting, etc., and at details of content of the image, in order to work out what it is really saying.

Ideally one should look at the signs and meaning in a range of visual formats, not only to reinforce the method but also to notice some of the repetitions – for example, the convention of smiling to the camera which permeates family albums as well as women's magazines.

If one wants to teach reading of image sequences – the structure and meaning in visual narrative – then comics provide a cheap and accessible source of material for looking at elements such as the use of close-ups or the structuring of a dramatic climax to carry the story from one week to another.

Covert messages

Analysis of material for its full meaning looks for the full range of messages, not just those on the surface. In the case of the media (and many other examples of communication) the important messages are those which make statements about values and beliefs. These value messages are usually more or less hidden. Advertisements, for instance, don't just sell a product or service, they sell beliefs and values to which the product is attached. Discovering these media messages may be a way in which one can point out how much media communication reinforces the way things are, and rarely talks about how things might be or should be.

Institution

Is mainly about ownership and finance of mass communication. The main thing is to explain who owns what – and to point out that this ownership adds up to dominant control of these major communication systems by relatively few multinational organizations. Then get over what this signifies in terms of potential influence and of choice for the audience. In terms of finance, the main thing to discuss is who pays for the systems of communication, for newspapers and programmes, or for books and records, and again to point up the significance of this. One should also discuss the influence of advertising as a source of revenue, and the attraction of large profits to a product-oriented market mentality.

Institutions have certain repetitious working practices and certain values they espouse. These practices and values come through in the product. In general one wants to get across the remarkable similarity in values and approach to creating product right across the media industries.

Product

Try to convey the idea that all the TV programmes, magazines, etc., can be seen as products because they are mass-produced and packaged to attract the audience, like a packet of cornflakes. They are like this because this is what gets ratings and profits in. But the effect is that a lot of the material is broadly similar, and doesn't offer that much choice to the audience.

Audience

Audiences are partly created by the institutions and the advertisers, and are partly there to be discovered, defined by some common denominator such as interests. The audience may be seen in the product. One can look at the nature of different audiences, at the ways in which they may be influenced by the messages, at their lack of access to the people who control the messages.

Pace the concept of 'mass', above, it is important to get over the idea that there are lots of large overlapping audiences, not one single mass audience.

Constraints

This is really about censorship and limitations on the production system of any one of the media. There are constraints of time, money and the law. There are also formal mechanisms of censorship – but the British media are almost entirely self-censored, not very effectively. So one can look at the way constraints may limit the range of what we get, and at the way that weak censorship allows, for example, newspapers to print lies, and advertising to continue to exploit women.

Practical simulation exercises will give some idea of what it is like to work to deadlines and within the expectations of a given genre or type of newspaper. Comparison of cinema and television versions of films will raise questions about how and why censorship is practised, in respect of what is or is not cut.

Representation

Look at the way types and social groups are represented throughout the media – in effect look at *stereotyping*. But go beyond describing characteristics – draw out the beliefs associated with these types, and the influence that this has on our ways of valuing the old, the disabled, the young, and other groupings.

An exercise in image analysis which involved annotating some magazine images with comments on the signs and their meanings, might well pinpoint signs of type and the value messages attached to these.

Mediation – selection and construction

This is the process through which original material is changed before it appears in print or on the screen. The most obvious example is news, but the same is true also, for instance, of drama. It is possible to look at a piece of a novel, or a news article, and then to consider how it would be handled on television. This says a lot about the medium and its conventions, about degrees to which truth may be distorted and the audience influenced in one way or another.

It is important to get across the idea that the non-fiction material of the media is as much a construct as any of the story forms. One then has to deal with questions such as who does the selecting? on what basis? with what intentions? and with what effects?

Genre

Catalogue the types of content in newspapers or types of programme on television. Then look at the combination of elements one expects to see in a genre – the formula. Again, not only get students to recognize and describe the elements of the formulae, but also get at the meanings of, for example, a soap – what is said about types, about social attitudes, about beliefs and values. Point out that because genres are popular, anything that they do put across is going to be influential. Point out that this influence is a result of the programme's popularity and the repetition of elements and ideas, both of which contribute to a reinforcement of meaning.

It is easy to fall into the trap of only reproducing the formula as part of a class exercise. This is fun and makes one a popular teacher. But being able to imitate any one of the media forms does not prove that a pupil has learnt anything about what is communicated through such a form and how. It is important to try rule-breaking exercises and to deconstruct examples of genre material, for example by carrying out a news presentation activity that deliberately breaks conventions of presentation and content. This kind of activity is good fun because it seems to send up the news, but is also actually very revealing.

Stereotypes

These are simplified notions of people divided by categories. This categorization is an integral part of perception. In the sense that it helps sort out information and external stimulus, there is nothing wrong with stereotyping *per se*. But as a concept it is often treated critically in media study because the categorizing remains limited and tends to promote unflattering views of people by gender, age, occupation, etc.

When teaching stereotyping it is most important to get beyond description to interpretation. It is all very well to conduct exercises which identify physical and even behavioural characteristics of types, but it is the attitudes and values associated with these characteristics which need to be brought into the open and debunked for the generalizations which they are.

Conventions

These are rules about what one expects to see and to read, and how one expects this content to be handled. Such rules help one anticipate the story line of a soap, but can also make the material tedious and repetitious. Imaginative genre material will break and remould some of its conventions precisely because it knows what the audience expects. Deal with the conventions of news for example – find out what one expects to see and how one expects it to be treated. Then get across the idea that these conventions may limit our view of the world.

News values

These are the conventions of news content and presentation – they are what the news machine values, thinks we should be told and knows how we should be told it. Again, get pupils to analyse and describe programmes and front pages so that these patterns are exposed. Then get across the idea that the fact of these partial values matters because we are only getting a version of the truth, and being asked to espouse values that are actually trivial (does it really matter if the Princess of Wales falls on her backside in the snow while on a ski-ing holiday?) For further information on 'news values' (in addition to regular monitoring of news services), see Dimbleby and Burton (1985) *More Than Words* (chapter 5); Masterman (1980), *Teaching About Television*, London: Macmillan; Cohen and Young (1987), *The Manufacture of News*, London: Constable; and Hartley (1982), *Understanding News*, London: Methuen.

Agenda-setting

The idea is that news organizations set up their topics based on an agenda of news items for a given week or month or more – they tell us what we ought to be interested in. Activities undertaken should sort out what the agenda is, and then ask questions as to why these items are on the agenda anyway (back to Princess Diana), as well as how they are kept there (e.g. by turning a news story into a long-running drama).

Realism

Especially with relation to film and television, it can be useful to look at realism. Inevitably one will be discussing conventions and representation. The important thing to get across is that there are various conventions of treatment, in particular, which define what a documentary is, and which convince us that it is telling the truth. One might deal similarly with the fictional mode of drama-documentary.

It is useful to describe the devices, but then to go on to see why they matter. Essentially this is because they persuade us to believe in what is being represented. In other words, it comes back again to influence and effects as well as to what is being said. This concept can be drawn out through practical work, storyboards, treatments, tape-slide or video.

Course plans

Finally, in this chapter we offer three examples of course plans, one for GCSE over one year of thirty weeks, one for BTEC National over two years, of sixty weeks, and one for A level, also over two years. These may not please everyone, but they should be useful as a framework, and they do provide examples of how the various elements of course content that we have described may be brought together. We have not restated the aims and objectives but are assuming that they are as stated in the published syllabuses, summary extracts of which can be found below in Chapter 5.

Students' responses to versions of these plans have been generally favourable, but of course they would not be 'delivered' exactly as printed here, since they are always adapted as a result of interaction and negotiation with students, and as a result of current events and issues and the availability of new materials.

Introduction

The layout for each of these three course plans is slightly different in each case, partly because of the nature of the course addressed, partly to provide some variety, but in all cases we have not presumed to provide too detailed a breakdown. Everyone works in different circumstances and will have to adapt these suggestions to suit their own timetable.

We have made the assumption that everyone wants to know which topic (and concept) might come in what order, and know what activities might be relevant and useful. Where activities or strategies are identified we have provided the barest indication of the background (to, for example, a simulation). Where concepts are identified separately they are either referred back to activities, or again there is a bare indication of the type of activity that might bring out such ideas.

GCSE course plan

This plan assumes a one-year course of twenty-seven weeks in real terms. It is broken down into half-termly units. It assumes four hours a week teaching time. If there is less time available, it seems likely that one would have to ask pupils to spend more of their own time working on projects, keeping class time strictly for consultation. It might also be necessary to ask that case studies, set up and reviewed in class, are otherwise completed in the pupils' own time. Each half-term of this plan is broken down under three headings: activities, concepts and projects. Because project and oral assessment comprises 50 per cent of the total for this syllabus (SEG mode 1), it is especially important to lock it into any course plan.

Autumn term block 1 – 6 weeks

Projects Introduce these after three weeks: explain the terms of reference; emphasize need for diary; discuss possible ideas; students to draft possible topics/aims/audience. (3 hours)

Activities A group task – based on the production of book pages designed to teach young children some simple maths concept.
This will give experience of problem-solving, of dealing with different means of communication, and will encourage co-operation. (2 hours)
A case study – based on making arrangements to invite people to some type of conference.
This could include a letter of invitation, a leaflet about the event, a map, and perhaps a schedule of activities drawn from notes. It would test various kinds of skill, including the ability to draw information from given materials. (3 hours)
Library work – an optional task in which pupils look at different reference sources for definitions of communication, and report back in groups.
The point of this activity would be to engage with study skills, including basic note-making, and to make a point about resources available. (1½ hours)
A group task – to design and produce a leaflet/booklet for new pupils, including research of existing information and of audience.
This would reinforce concepts being taught, be used to teach them, help prepare for the project, give experience of sustained work (7 hours)
Individual task – to produce a message in different mediums warning householders that their water supply would be cut off for a period of time.
This would make a point about the qualities of different forms of communication. (1½ hours)

Concepts Forms and qualities of communication – build a grid to define examples in terms of elements such as permanence, cheapness of production, visualization. (1 hour)
Uses of communication – look at examples in various forms and media to illustrate different uses. (1 hour)
Process and basic concepts – use various packets and labels to illustrate these and to make sense of basic models. (4 hours)

Autumn term block 2 – 6 weeks

Projects Topics and terms of reference to be registered with the teacher by November. The structure and pattern of record-keeping for the log to be established. Research into the topic and into the audience knowledge and needs to be conducted. Provide appropriate help with method and keep a record of progress. (6 hours)

Activities Interview simulations – one modelled on a chat show, one on a job interview.
These should be used to bring out points about process, the use of non-verbal communication, strategies, conventions in social interaction. (4 hours)

Case situation – based on experience of a part-time worker, concerned with breakdowns in communication.
To make points about attitude and disagreement about meaning as contributing to problems in a work situation. (2 hours)

Role plays – based on everyday home, leisure, and school experience.
To illustrate barriers to communication, and types of positive and negative verbal and non-verbal behaviour which encourage or discourage relationships. (3 hours)

Individual task – based on obtaining information from the publicity sections of local organizations.
This would involve making a telephone call to the chosen organization, making a visit if necessary, obtaining information on paper if necessary, then making a short presentation to the class about the topic, accompanied by a handout fact sheet which the student has to prepare. This includes two types of interaction for later discussion, and provides experience of presentation to a group. It will be necessary to spread the available time across a period of two weeks. (4 hours)

Simulation – based on a department store complaints department, with those manning it dealing with various types of customer and problem.
This would bring out points about good perception and effective communication. (3 hours)

Concepts Notionally, there are only 2 hours remaining. We would argue that these concepts could be integrated with the above. Alternatively, the role plays might be dispensed with. Some separate short activities relating to the concepts are suggested.

Communication needs:

Self-image and self-esteem – try using literary passages and women's magazine source material.

Perception – compare notes made on people observed, under given headings.

Non-verbal communication – including description of types of behaviour.

Interpersonal skills – group exercises to prepare short pieces showing how we warn, persuade, attract others.

What does one teach?

Conventions:
Meaning – play a piece of radio news, ask for notes on this, and compare the results for agreement on what was said and meant.

Spring term block 1 – 6 weeks

Projects Students should be keeping a regular log. They should complete the bulk of their project work, including making layouts, and producing drafts for checking by and discussion with the teacher. Methods of testing opinions on the effectiveness of the finished communication should be sorted out. (12 hours)

Activities Simulation – based on the idea of a group of friends trying to organize a holiday.
To bring out ideas about role and about constructive and obstructive behaviour. (2 hours)
Case study – based on the idea of a club or students' union committee that is trying to raise funds, and is having meetings about this.
This covers formats such as notice of meeting, agenda, etc., and is designed to precede the simulation. (2 hours)
Simulation – an extension of the above.
Designed to teach formal group experience (committees), including information in the profiles so that everyone has a piece to say to the rest of the committee. Concepts relating to groups, group behaviour, conventions of communication, can also be dealt with through this. (3 hours)
Multi-task – based on obtaining information, in small groups, about charities.
This would deal covertly with co-operation and decision-making, and overtly with the tasks/formats, which could include a poster, a circular letter, and a display advertisement. Given time, these publicity efforts could be compared with what these organizations actually produce. (4 hours)

Concepts Again it is assumed that these would be largely or wholly integrated within the above. Alternatively, for example, the multi-task could be reduced to a 2-hour case study.
Types of groups.
Characteristics of groups.
Role and behaviour in groups.
Communication patterns in groups: including models.

Spring term block 2 – 5 weeks

Projects These should be completed by the end of March for marking in April. Associated oral examinations to be completed by

23 April. Any testing of project achievements also to be completed. A student commentary dealing with project method and success also to be completed. (10 hours)

Activities Image analysis – based on magazine and newspaper advertisements.
This would bring out points about signification and meaning in particular, also about source, audience, persuasion. (3 hours)
Group task – to compare and contrast programme schedules for ITV/BBC.
This would bring out points about programme types, programming, audience, general information about the BBC and ITV operations and institutions. (3 hours)
Content analysis – of examples from the popular and quality press.
This would bring out points about structures and types of content, the reasons for these, and the selection/construction/values inherent in the news operation. (4 hours)

Concepts Communication process.
Signs and meaning.
Selection and construction.

Summer term – 4 weeks

Projects and orals are completed. Centre marks will have been sent in by 1 May. The first examination will take place in the middle of May. We do not propose revision time. If anything is to be checked it would be simply the key aspects of process. These can act as a check for Paper 2 – i.e. what is the audience for any of the given communication tasks? They are also relevant to Paper 1 in that understanding of these will be tested more or less overtly.

Activities Storyboard – based on the titles sequence for a television programme.
This will not only provide experience of design and visualization, it will also teach something about use of the medium, about visual narrative and about typical content of the type of programme chosen. (3 hours)
Case study – based on the idea of starting local community radio, or perhaps on a local hospital broadcasting service.
This could include a segment of script, a press release, a new station logo, or even a short report on local circumstances and local needs. (3 hours)
Simulation – based on the idea of an advertising agency team and their clients discussing a possible campaign.

What does one teach?

This would bring out ideas about persuasion, audience, means of communication, possible effects, what a campaign is. (3 hours)
Key questions – on two examples of TV genres viewed.
To bring out points about the formula, use of stereotypes, characteristics of genre, the importance of genres as product. (2 hours)
Treatment – one to complete from an example started and based on a genre episode.
To bring out points about narrative, conventions, expectations, television output. (2 hours)
Content analysis – of girls' and boys' comics.
To bring out points about stereotypes, repetition, values, the construction of meaning, possible effects. (3 hours)

Concepts Genre, stereotypes, conventions, narrative.
Communication and meaning.

BTEC National – People in Organizations

This course plan starts from the premise that you have some idea of BTEC requirements. So you will have the skills statement to hand, to relate this to the activities which follow. You will be capable of running a grid checklist to make sure that the skills have been adequately covered, as we believe they have. You will be aware that part-time students may need an adapted version of a full-time course. You will know that the exact nature of assessment is negotiable, and so one may or may not assume end-of-year assessment, whether or not through a formal examination. You will understand that the extent of integration of core modules is also flexible. You will know that there is in effect a course content defined in terms of skills/activities required as course experience for students, combined with a range of formats appropriate to business career aspirations.

We are dealing with students who are supposed to have covered the equivalent of A level by the end of the course, and who therefore can cope with explanation and interpretation of the concepts behind the activities and skills. The degree of abstraction and theorizing is a matter for you to decide. The point of the course is certainly to equip the students to function well in their working environment, but there has to be some explanation of why tasks are required of the students. Otherwise they become activities undertaken for their own sake, performance without understanding.

The following breakdown is in segments, term by term. Each segment is based on an activity, with an accompanying statement of the topic or concept behind the activity, if this is not perfectly obvious. A number of activities are marked down as assignments for assessment. Remember that students can be referred for individual assignments, and make another attempt on those skills, but they cannot be referred at the end of a year, when they will have been deemed in toto *to have achieved a distinction, a merit, a pass or a fail. Some activities are group ones, others individual: appropriate assessment methods need to be adopted. A range of relevant formats is referred to in this plan.*

It will be seen that some of the activities duplicate skills. This is not necessarily spelled out. The assumption is that there is no harm in reinforcement. It is assumed that there will always be some kind of feedback on activities and tasks. We take it that all task sheets should include at least a summary of the criteria of achievement for each of the three pass categories. Some of the activities require work outside the institution. We have not prescribed visits of various kinds, though these are obviously possible.

Year 1 – Autumn term

Introduction – problem-solving games in groups to illustrate the importance of co-operation and communication. Exercises to cover study skills such as time management, note-making, reading, use of resources in the institution.

Case study (assignment) – based on the organization of a business conference.
To cover formats such as a schedule, a letter, a map. To bring out points about common principles of and factors in communication.

Role plays – based on mini-situations such as welcoming the client, making arrangements for a meeting, dealing with a difficult customer, dealing with an employee with problems, and leading up to progress interviews, including a discussion of criteria for these. *To bring out points about self, perception of others, strategies, uses of non-verbal communication, interpersonal skills.*

Case situations (assignment) – providing examples of types of barrier to communication in work situations, demanding a written solution to the problems described, as well as brief presentation of solutions to the whole group.
To cover common problems in communication, including poor perception and conflicting attitudes, as well as effective interpersonal communication.

What does one teach?

Year 1 – Spring term

Simulation: groups and decision-making – set in the context of an ailing small company and the various options that may save it from extinction.
This will reprise problem-solving methods, bring out points about effective co-operation, about roles, about constructive and obstructive communication in groups, and could use small group models to discuss effective decision-making structures.

Case study (assignment) – referring to a meeting of the Board of Directors of the above company.
To cover documentation relating to business meetings: notice of, agenda for, minutes of last meeting, etc.

Simulation (assignment) – the conduct of the above meeting.
To bring out points about the proper conduct of a formal meeting. To bring out points about effective participation and positive communication behaviour.

Case situations: using the telephone – set in various backgrounds such as telephone selling.
To bring out points about effective and ineffective uses of this device, with the option of reinforcement through some group activity such as designing a wallchart on the subject for display in the office.

Organizations and models – descriptive of vertically integrated and other structures.
To raise points about organizations as information-handling systems, and about the variously effective structures for carrying out this function.

Case situations – representing breakdowns of communication in small and large organizations, in the manufacturing and service sectors.
To bring out points about formal channels and the grapevine, about gatekeeping, about human and mechanical reasons for breakdowns within networks.

Year 1 – Summer

Investigative exercise (assignment) – based on given types of organization with varying needs: to look into machines and systems covering the areas of word-processing, microcomputing, Fax transmission, information networks, databases. The task

50

would be to produce a summary chart with commentary covering types, availability, maintenance, applications, advantages and disadvantages, and finally recommendations.

The point of the exercise, which could easily be conducted in pairs, is to obtain and share up-to-date information about information technology, as well as to practise information-gathering skills, and representation of information.

Investigative exercise (assignment) – dealing with social effects and perceptions of information technology with relation to work and leisure. The substance of this would be the construction, administration, and processing of a questionnaire relating to public knowledge of and attitudes towards the subject, supplemented by local authority statistics. The assignment would lead not only to a graphic presentation of findings, but also to an oral presentation to the group.

The point of this exercise is to cover the topic and the experience of the formats. It could also encompass subsidiary topics and information such as employment patterns and conditions, health and safety at work, the Data Protection Act and its implications.

Practical work – depending on time available, this could cover hands-on items such as word-processing, use of databases, and use of spreadsheets. The scope and individual nature of such exercises depends on resources.

Year 2 – Autumn

Case study (assignment) – a detailed profile of a company, describing its structure, as well as certain trading and growth problems that it has. The materials should cover areas such as sales and marketing, purchasing, stock control, wages and production. The task will be to produce a report on the company's problems, with graphic appendices where appropriate. Because of the next assignment there must be feedback discussion and agreement by the whole group on the nature of the problems.

Apart from covering the format, formal and informal organizational structure, and the other topics referred to, this activity should also include reference to relevant legislation and a reprise of models and organizational barriers to communication.

Role play – with the above as assumed background: to enact progress, redeployment, redundancy interviews.

To reprise and develop interpersonal skills, including awareness of perception and feedback.

Simulation (assignment) – also drawn from the company and situation described. A negotiation exercise between management and unions concerned with new conditions, structures and pay scales. *To develop group skills: to deal with the management of conflict: also to engage with topics such as job satisfaction, health and safety at work, the working environment, motivation, working relationships.*

Year 2 – Spring

Case situation (assignment) – based on industrial consultants' report which contrasts systems of organization and management styles. The task is to make a written evaluation of these in terms of efficiency, satisfaction, and their various merits. *To bring out points about the following topics: company organization, management style, defining efficiency, systems analysis, managing change.*

Hands-on activities – short tasks based on circulating groups to provide experience of data-processing, desktop publishing, word-processing, electronic mail, viewdata, faxing, spreadsheets.

Simulation exercise (assignment) – in general to deal with job interviews. In particular, have a preparatory activity stage in which members of various groups compose letters of application and response, display advertisements, job descriptions, curricula vitae. Then have a simulation stage in which interviews are conducted in role, with follow-up evaluation, preferably (as with other exercises) with video-recording to review.

Year 2 – Summer

Publicity task (assignment) – based on research into an existing organization in the commercial or public sector, and an evaluation of their existing publicity material. The end task will be to prepare a (revised) leaflet or booklet based on the critique and on some consumer research. *Apart from the format and the experience of research and evaluation, this final activity will reinforce general communication principles and factors in the communication process.*

AEB A Level Communication Studies

This plan assumes a two-year course of approximately thirty weeks in each year at five hours per week. It is not our intention to provide a rigid week-by-week guide since our approach based on specific

Figure 2.4 Communication Studies A Level. An integrated study of human communication

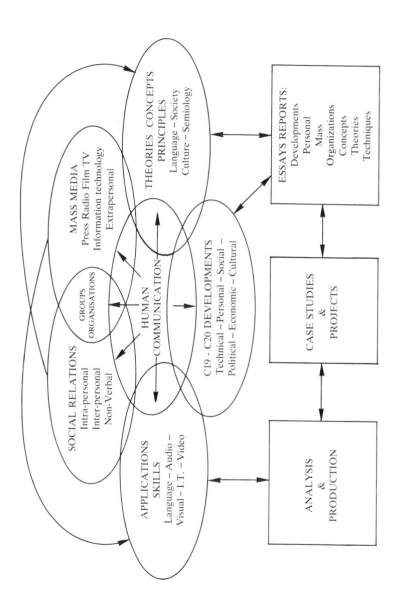

needs and contexts may not suit your situation. We simply want to draw broad brushstrokes of general strategy which you may find helpful in making your own plans. There is a note of topic areas, potential resources and student activities. At the end are more details of the books and other resources which are mentioned.

Term 1: printed and broadcast media

Week No	Topic/Activity/Concepts	Resources
1	Introduction to course: aims, syllabus, expectations, methods. Why study communications? Your commitment – contract of learning. Group and pair discussions.	Questionnaires
	Group exercise: building something.	Lego or cardboard
2/3	What do we mean by communication? Library search – different disciplinary perspectives. *Book-reading assignments* – presentation of review as one side of A4 paper for noticeboard. Study skills: techniques of reading, note-making, presentation including graphical use of IT – word-processing.	Library classification sheet
4/5	Introduction to print media in United Kingdom newspapers and magazines: range of titles, styles, purposes, audiences – notions of market/audience. *Magazine assignment: analysis and presentation* Introduction to report-writing and use of overhead projector for oral presentations.	*Willings Press Guide*
6	Individuals' short (5-minute) presentations on magazine findings.	
7	Debriefing on magazines: issues of image analysis, advertising techniques. Introduction to models – basic linear aim/medium/audience/ effect/feedback. Activity of creating linear models for different media and different situations.	*Talking Pictures* slide/ tape Morgan and Welton O'Sullivan McQuail

8/9/10	*Simple video-camera group – assignment based on local events/places.* Planning of storyboard and production.	Video equipment
11	Broadcast TV: analysis of techniques in different genres. Current broadcasting institutions: BBC, IBA, satellite, cable; international comparisons.	BBC. IBA leaflets News stories
12	*Case study from 1986 exam paper.* Scheduling analysis from Radio and TV Times. *Scheduling exercise: plan a night's or week's viewing (adapt Masterman).*	Bethell tapes Dimbleby and Burton
13	Class monitoring of week's programmes. Mass-media models. Seek studio visit/museum visit/IBA gallery. TV advertising: theme of conscious communication technique.	Morley Masterman Alvarado Root
14	Advertising campaigns (linear models). Guest speaker – advertising agency?	Campaign sheets Campaign magazines

Term 2: advertising/news/language

1/2/3	*Group advertising assignment: selling a chocolate bar* – storyboard/poster/ magazine advert/audio or video advert. Analysis of advertising in various media. Controls on advertising. *Essay on advertising topics.*	Bethell Dyer Myers ASA
4	Termly book-reading assignment: select book on topics of current concern to course (i.e. media, advertising, news). Noticeboard review presentations.	
5	Introduction to language studies. Concepts: language, linguistics, code, sign, semiotics.	Montgomery

6	Varieties of language – taped and printed. Student examples from various sources – gobbledegook, fiction, non-fiction, legal, newspapers, etc.	
7/8	*Analysis of one day's newspapers:* topics, treatment, language, photos, readers . . . Newspaper simulation – front page. Newspaper ownership and statistics of sales. Local newspapers – what role? Visit by local reporter.	Hartley Cohen & Young Baistow Glasgow Media Group
10	Devise questionnaire for survey on news – Introduction to design of questionnaire.	
11	Analysis of questionnaire findings. *Essay on 'News'.*	
12	Briefing for mini-projects next term. Outline of possibilities for planning contacts over Easter.	

Term 3: mini-projects/review/preview

1/2/3	*Group project work in selected media* – audio/slide/tape/video/ photography/print. Opportunities for individual interviews for course progress review.	McKeown
4	Presentation of projects and self-reflection/review.	
5	Review of year: consolidation of topics.	
6	End-of-year assessments/ examinations.	
7/8	Preview of second year: project planning. Future plans: opportunities for communication and media studies careers and higher education.	

Term 4: projects/interpersonal communication/radio

1	Plans for year 2: review of year 1 and topics for second year. Project ideas update leading to completion of registration forms.	
2/3/4/5/6	Simulation/role plays for group work leading to concepts of IPC: interaction, transaction, roles, intra-personal issues, self-concept, perception, self-presentation. Termly book assignment on IPC. These concepts explored through group games and analysis of video materials and slides. Observation activities for NVB in different social contexts.	Burton and Dimbleby Argyle Myers and Myers
7	IPC models of communication for situations. *Essay on interpersonal communication.*	Fiske Patton and Giffin
8	Role-play interviews. Listening case study (1983 examination).	
9	Projects review for progress.	
10/11/12	Radio unit: current and past broadcasting/roles of radio as a changing medium – international, national, local, and community dimensions. Local radio presenter/visit.	Crisell
13	*Group assignment to produce audio tape*: 10 minutes of magazine programme.	

Term 5: communication in organizations

1/2	*Assignment for communication audit of college or other organizations:* formal and informal channels, variety of business documents. Project progress reviews.
3	Meeting simulation for decision-making/role-playing – e.g. motorway route enquiry.

Figure 2.5 Model for main elements in a communication course

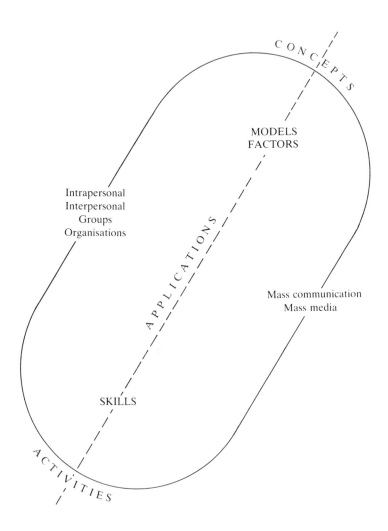

4/5	Case studies of business procedures – e.g. appointing staff (job analysis, job specification, advertisement, selection, interview).	Evans Dimbleby and Burton Myers and Myers
6/7/8	Business external relations: images of an organization – use of public relations and strategies (press releases, corporate image).	MacShane
9/10	Case study simulation: 'sell your region' or business relocation.	
11/12	Management styles – theories of organizations related to individual experiences. Revision of course and preparation for examinations – review of models of communication.	McQuail

Term 6: review and examination preparation

Revision of course. Individual analysis of strengths and weaknesses for personal revision. Essay planning and writing for Paper 1. Case study work for Paper 2. Project oral assessments.

Resources The notes of resources above refer to the following materials which we have found useful. The general resource lists in Chapter 6 provide additional sources of information and learning materials. The place of publication is London unless otherwise indicated.

Advertising campaign materials – see p. 111ff.
Alvarado, M., Gutch, R. and Wollen, T. (1987) *Learning the Media*, Macmillan.
Argyle, M. (1987) *Bodily Communication*, Methuen.
———— (1983) *The Psychology of Interpersonal Behaviour*, Penguin.
Baistow, T. (1985) *Fourth Rate Estate: An Anatomy of Fleet Street*, Comedia.
Bethell, A. (1987) *The Media Tapes*, Methuen.
Burton, G., and Dimbleby, R. (1988) *Between Ourselves: An Introduction to Interpersonal Behaviour*, Edward Arnold.
Cohen, S., and Young, J. (1987) *The Manufacture of News*, Constable.
Crisell, A. (1986) *Understanding Radio*, Methuen.
Dimbleby, R., and Burton, C. (1985) *More Than Words: An Introduction to Communication*, Methuen.
Dyer, G. (1982) *Advertising as Communication*, Methuen.
Evans, D. (1987) *People, Communication and Organisations*, Pitman.
Fiske, J., (1982) *Introduction to Communication Studies*, Methuen.

What does one teach?

Glasgow University Media Group (1982) *Really Bad News*, Writers and Readers Publishing Cooperative.

Hartley, J. (1982) *Understanding News*, Methuen.

McKeown, N. (1982) *Case Studies and Projects in Communication*, Methuen.

McQuail, D. (1983) *Mass Communication Theory*, Sage.

McQuail, D., and Windahl, S. (1981) *Communication Models for the Study of Mass Communication*, Longman.

MacShane, D. (1979) *Using the Media: how to deal with the press, radio and television*, Pluto.

Masterman, L. (1980) *Teaching About Television*, Macmillan.

Montgomery, M. (1986) *Introduction to Language and Society*, Methuen.

Morgan, J., and Welton, P. (1986) *See What I Mean: An Introduction to Visual Communication*, Edward Arnold.

Morley, D., and Whitaker, B. (1983) *Press, Radio and Television: An Introduction to the Media*, Comedia.

Myers, G.E., and Myers, M.T. (1986) *The Dynamics of Human Communication*, McGraw-Hill.

Myers, K. (1986) *Understains . . . The Sense and Seduction of Advertising*, Comedia.

O'Sullivan, T., *et al* (1983) *Key Concepts in Communication*, Methuen.

Patton, B., and Giffin, K. (1977) *Interpersonal Communication in Action*, Harper & Row.

Root, J. (1986) *Open the Box*, Comedia.

Talking Pictures (slide/tape), 1980 – for details see p. 148.

Willings Press Guide, published annually.

Chapter three

How does one teach?

Some grandmothers have a fine egg collection carefully sucked and preserved. But we are also aware that there are a number of teachers who, in speaking of communication work, will say, that is all very well in principle, but how do you actually teach it? 'It', of course, is many things on a communication course. How does one teach interpersonal skills, the concepts of sign and meaning, or any kind of practical work? How does one relate theory to practice?

We will do our best to answer these questions, providing some practical examples of tasks. We cannot cover every topic on your course, but we can suggest various approaches which can be adapted to cover all eventualities. In the end, you will teach the way that best suits you, your situation, and your pupils, but we hope that what follows will provide every reader with a few ideas, and some material that they can actually use.

Theory – practice

One problem that all teachers have is whether to start with the ideas and then put them into practice, or whether to start with some practical activity and then point out the principles and concepts which this illustrates. We prefer a mixture of the two, arguing that a variety of methods not only allows for some useful repetition and reinforcement of learning but is also more interesting for teacher and student alike. Obviously, too much standing in front of a class and making an exposition of ideas and their applications will pall in the end, however riveting the delivery. Equally there is a danger in the total activity approach, that the practice becomes an end in itself, and the student finds it difficult to then move to a level of abstraction, and even resents having to theorize after having enjoyed an activity. (Not that one has to theorize about every activity in communication.)

However, it needs to be said firmly that there is a principle at

Figure 3.1 Three-part model to describe learning in communication work

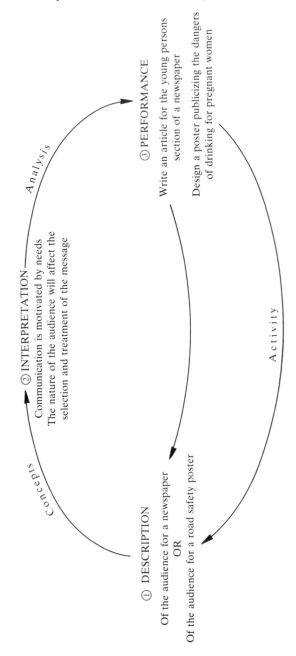

stake. That, for example, not only should a communication student be able to grasp the idea that all examples of communication are examples of process, with identifiable parts to this whole, but should also grasp that their creation of communication should be informed by understanding of the same basic parts (concepts). They can describe meanings and audience with relation to the mass media, they can decode the message: they can also be conscious of how they construct meanings in their own communication, and can take into account the profile and needs of their chosen audience.

The Communications Kit by Weston and Banks (to be published in 1989, in Cambridge) exemplifies the activity-led approach in which students may undertake units of work through which they learn ideas and skills, but this does not preclude the need for and value of that input which is exposition at the right point. This is also the guiding principle behind the preferred approach to BTEC People in Organizations. On the other hand, especially when a distinct unit of work has to be set up (see previous course plans), there is an argument for making a plain explanation of essential ideas and their importance before proceeding to practical exercises which reinforce these ideas and introduce other concepts. Many students like to know why they are doing what they are doing – indeed, we would argue that it is vital, given the breadth of this subject, to keep on checking with students as to what is on the agenda and what they are meant to be learning. In addition, it is often the case that students find it difficult to cope with theoretical information in bits and pieces. They will take an initial explanation on face value, especially if its applications are briefly illustrated. This part of the theoretical input may acquire greater coherence for being delivered intact. It can always be reviewed at the end of a given unit, to ensure understanding.

In short, we are opting for a mixed economy. And we would emphasize a point made in the last chapter – that even with a syllabus that emphasizes skills learning and practical work, one often needs to offer some kind of theory in order to unify and justify that procedure.

Communication theory

Since this is what most vexes teachers when trying to think about how to teach, it may be worth reminding ourselves of what we mean by the phrase anyway. Theory is about explanations of how and why communication takes place. It is dominated by the notion of process and of signs and meanings. On one level it is about teaching terms, factors, or concepts (interchangeable words) summarized in a word or phrase. These terms may be descriptive of parts of the process, and they may lead to interpretation. On a basic level this interpretation is about how meanings are created, how they may affect us, what makes for effective communication, and what impedes communication.

Theory is also about models and the creation of models. These are graphic representations of process and the relationship of its parts. Theory is also about principles – statements incorporating terms, and offering some apparent truth about what affects communication. It could be said that these principles are propositions that have been set up, tested, and found to be valid as far as we can see. One old favourite is that which proposes that communication is irreversible – things once said cannot be unsaid, only modified.

Theory is also about issues, debates concerning messages and their significance. Usually these issues fall within the areas of mass communication and new technology. For example, one such issue is whether new technology is so far facilitating the production of newspapers that it will create more choice for the public, or whether it is simply making it easier for a few people to make a lot of money.

Team teaching – individual teaching

The issue of how to teach is not just concerned with devices for delivering experience, skills, and ideas. It has to do with resources. These resources include people as well as equipment, finance, and other facilities. It is difficult to do small group work with a class of thirty and no spare space to spill into. We will allude to these problems, and try not to suggest ideas that are expensive or mechanically difficult.

The question of who teaches is an issue in itself, especially if one is preparing to take on a communication course, or if a situation is prescribed (perhaps through the ways in which YTS or CPVE are handled). As things stand, probably some 70 per cent of those teaching communication are English teachers by training. But there is no law of nature which particularly fits English teachers to this task. One could argue that a background in psychology or even anthropology would be just as useful. Where background does become relevant is if one proposes to team-teach communication. Lack of experience or lack of confidence often persuades an institution and those taking on the task that it would be a good idea to share the responsibility. There are good reasons for doing this, if indeed the experience of a group of people can be brought together.

But some words of warning. It is no good wheeling in the person who teaches photography on the assumption that they can do a bit of visual communication. They may well do what they have always done – and this will not help pupils unravel the meanings in images. Team teaching needs co-ordination, and co-ordination demands a co-ordinator and time for meetings. If you cannot get or give this, then teams are likely to be as problematic as individuals. Precisely because communication does have a core of theory and integrates theory with practice, it is necessary to have fairly tight control of what is going on. Otherwise the course will fall apart into bits and pieces which the students cannot bring together in any meaningful way.

It is true, on the other hand, that the single teacher can hold together what is happening and when. This person can make decisions to let a piece of practical work run on, and no colleagues will be inconvenienced. However, we would not wish for the sole class teacher approach to be promoted carelessly. The most obvious problem is that this person has got to have real commitment to their task. They have to teach and train themselves into competence in the various areas of the subject. It can be a burdensome obligation. One cannot, in this position, say that one will not teach storyboards because 'I'm not good on visuals'. Perhaps an ideal but long-term compromise is to build up enough communication work and staff so that some kind of sharing mixed with sole responsibility for a group is no longer a problem.

We will now get down to the nuts and bolts of various methodologies used by teachers in general, and by communication teachers in particular. We will relate these to at least some of the content areas described in the last chapter. It is one of the pleasures of communication work that it does lend itself so readily to varieties of approach – varieties of group and practical work in particular.

Teaching topics: a selection

Communication theory

Having indicated what theory includes, the next question is, how does one teach it? There are several approaches, all of which presuppose that theoretical explanations and frameworks should not be separate from the actual practice of communication. We are not advocating the learning of theoretical perspectives for their own sakes, but rather as a means of analysing communication texts and acts, and of producing more effective pieces of communication.

First, and most simply, you can introduce concepts, issues and models through some form of direct presentation. So long as expositions are kept brief and are illustrated through familiar examples, then they can be effective and economic in terms of time and

Figure 3.2 General model for theory and topics within communication study

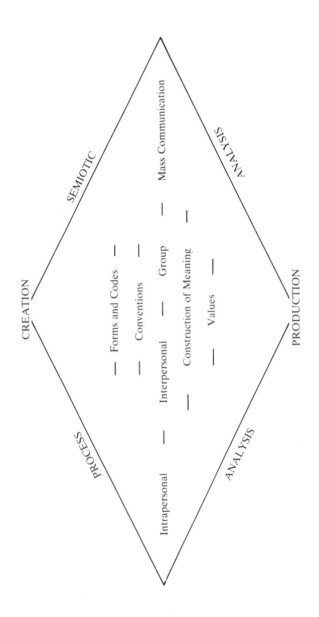

resources. There is nothing wrong with straightforward explanation at the right time and in the right way (a fact endorsed by our own students). It is essential to use a flipchart or overhead projector in order to display and discuss models. In the same way one may use visual mnemonics to explain, say, gatekeeping through drawings of gates or of funnels for agenda setting, backed up by notes on the day's newspapers with their selection of stories and angles on those stories.

Second, one can begin from actual situations or texts to draw out ideas and issues. Basic concepts of process such as purpose, content, selection and use of media, intended audience, intended effects on that audience, can all be described and analysed from that source material. Similarly such concepts can be invoked when planning the production of something as simple as a letter, an oral presentation or even an essay.

With regard to models, the familiar and limited linear models have been much used in textbooks, often as if they are the only explanation of communication processes. But process needs to take account of feedback, of context, of the co-relation of past experience and present communication (see *More Than Words*). If one represents a model of process including these ideas, then it can be made 'real' by writing under the terms the relevant elements in a conversation and in the transmission of a television programme. Another stimulus can be to use the example of pre-speech children (something within pupils' experience), and ask them to report observations on how the communication of such children is affected by their apparent needs, by context, how they give feedback, and so on.

The semiotic approach of engaging with levels of meaning in the production and reading of a text is less well represented. Without necessarily needing to use all the terminology, it is very possible to explore the concepts in different models and the notion of identifying signs and reading meanings, through something as familiar as breakfast cereal packets. A class collection of different packets can be used to raise questions about the significance of elements such as the following: packaging (box or bag); shapes; colours; impact; own brand or brand names; product names; verbal text (vocabulary, tone, style); visuals (cartoons, logos, illustrations); design concepts (layout); content (matters of information and attitude); intended audiences; persuasive techniques. All these would lead one to discussion of basics such as purpose, message, and audience, as well as to consideration of how the package as text was produced, why, and how it might be read. One would be able to put across the idea that there are signifiers in all forms of communication. One should be able to show that meaning goes beyond that which is represented on a physical level, and even beyond some obvious symbolism. There could even be questions raised about the very notion of breakfast, let alone the connotations of health and success suggested by many packets.

It is worth bearing in mind that there is that theory which is general and that which is particular to communication categories and topics. We have been dealing with the general. Particular concepts are referred to in the following sections.

Groups and communication

In the first place, the experience of working with others is a valuable one, so group work can be set up at any point in the course. For example, one could simply break the class into sub-groups, with case situations to discuss, and ask them to report back after a certain time. In this case, groups and communication are not the subject, but group work is the method.

If one does want to make groups both the object and the method of study, then the following activities could be useful for making the points which are commented on with relation to each example. You will have to make your own mind up as to how much you can fit into your course. It is possible to make many points about group characteristics and communication behaviour from just one group exercise.

Start with a problem-solving group activity – we have tried one in which the groups have to design and build a cardboard castle. It is surprising what a purposeful and even competitive atmosphere builds up. The general point that you may draw out of this is that groups get things done by pooling ideas and sharing tasks. You would hope to be able to make points about the phases through which a group bonds, roles displayed, the problem solving sequence, and the fact that co-operators succeed. You may well also see something about leadership styles – autocratic or democratic.

Magazine pictures can be collected and cut out to stimulate discussion about what types of groups there are and why people join groups.

Video recordings of groups, preferably of specific subculture examples, however garnered, can be used successfully to illustrate and discuss concepts such as group identity, norms, roles and the relationship of communication and culture to these.

Try a simulation exercise, for example one for a community council group meeting on an informal basis, with profiles designed to encourage examples of constructive and obstructive communication. One should be able to get down to specific verbal and non-verbal phrases which do things like encourage and invite others, or lock them out and reject them.

If one wants simply to check group concepts/characteristics such as task and goal to make the point that all groups have these in common, then a simple grid-filling exercise will work. A similar direct approach can be used by presenting and discussing models of small group networks, *vis-à-vis* decision-making. Students can be asked to draw their own sociometric models, after the purpose and design has been explained – and these make some attractive display material relating to who communicates with whom and how often. By this stage it is also important to be able to make clear what is different about group communication as opposed to one to one interaction.

Finally, a simulation of a more formal group interaction in a meeting provides a structured experience, something which relates to organizations, something which prepares students, one hopes, for later social skills, and which enables one to demonstrate all the previous ideas in action. Most of all it should be possible to see that conventions also operate in group situations and that there are communication skills to be learned and used in this aspect of our communication experience.

Non-verbal behaviour (NVB) and non-verbal communication (NVC)

Before saying anything about teaching this topic it is worth sorting out the distinction between these two terms. NVB is the more general term, used to include unconscious and unintentional behaviour. We cannot stop behaving. We cannot stop communicating. This is certainly true in the sense that people will read meanings into our behaviour, whether we like it or not. One may not intend to behave nervously at a formal interview, but it is likely that some of our behaviour in this situation will be interpreted as signs of nervousness. There may be a range of unconscious non-verbal behaviours such as sweating, dry throat, awkward gestures, stumbling over words, which we may enact in such a situation. These are involuntary acts. But we may also seek to control our behaviour consciously: we could choose to operate signs such as a taut sitting posture with tonus, making eye contact and smiling. In this case it may be said that the intention makes it communication (NVC).

NVC is the use of non-verbal behaviour as a means of communication, and includes the notion of decoding the NVC of others. In this context it is worth noting that developing social communication skills is largely a matter of making our non-verbal behaviours more controlled. Social conventions permit relatively spontaneous behaviour in children, but require adults to be able to communicate, to present themselves socially and to respond appropriately to others.

Having made these conceptual distinctions we now want to indicate ways of enabling students to read and to use non-verbal cues more effectively. NVC, popularly summarized through the term 'body language', is a good motivator of students' interest. If we are teachers of younger age groups in particular, we have to build on the attraction this topic has for those who are generally very concerned about how they appear to other people and who like to talk about this.

Teenage magazines for girls are a useful source of material, especially as they often run articles on body language or closely-related topics. Although these may be partial and superficial from an academic point of view, they provide a good starting point through these articles, and indeed through the illustrations. They are often concerned with social interaction and what may be termed 'people watching'. You will find that the most popular book of this type is called *Manwatching* (London: Triad Paperbacks, 1977), by Desmond Morris.

Having led into description of non-verbal behaviours, and discussion of the uses of non-verbal communication, it may then be a good thing to encourage students to do some 'manwatching' of their own. Observation within a framework which you provide in order to define what should be observed and recorded is an effective way of learning how and why people use NVC.

A refinement of this is to video-record interactions (either role-played or taken in some suitable location). These can be played back with the use of pause, replay, slow motion, sound down and so on. Any professional examples of dramatic interaction for which you have play rights are also useful in the same way. One can arrest the bewildering flow of non-verbal signs and break them down, look at the exchange of signs, and see how much meaning is conveyed even without speech. One can examine how interaction is predicted and controlled by the ways in which participants use non-verbal communication.

At the simplest level one can make sense of such behaviour by drawing out lists of its types and uses. For more advanced students there are established conventions for recording interactions – making analysis of conversations for example, but for most of our purposes this is not necessary. One wishes to describe what is seen in a structured way, and then interpret its significance in terms of purpose and effect, with relevance to perception and social interaction.

Role plays and simulations also provide an active approach to this topic. One can use observers (as well as a video camera if possible) primed to notice details such as how people interrupt, or how group members persuade others to their point of view. Obviously these strategies will only be successful when the class members are fairly relaxed and confident with one another. Some would argue that these activities help them into this relationship. And trust games (see *The Gamesters' Handbook*) can also be useful to bring out particular points about body space and eye contact.

So one may talk about description, in terms of defining a taxonomy of non-verbal behaviour for one's students, but then one also has to interpret this behaviour. Interpretation relates to other topics such as the relationship of NVC to speech, where, for example, it can be used to reinforce or to exaggerate the point of what is being said. It may also relate topics such as that of perception, where a great deal of our evaluation of others' attitudes and attributes is based on observation of their NVB. Or again, a good deal of the identity of subcultural groups is conveyed through their non-verbal communication. So this topic is one that may be dealt with on its own, but also one that will inevitably appear with relation to many aspects of the study of communication.

Genre

This is a fundamental concept and topic in terms of teaching mass communication. Both economic and cultural conditions converge in genre material. It can be argued that a majority of media material may be described as genre, with all that this implies in terms of mass production and social values. What is implied becomes the argument for teaching the topic. It could be said that one is trying to deal with three things, on one level or another. The first is simply the meaning of the term. Then there are the associated concepts and characteristics of genre material, their meanings and applications: these would include repetition and reinforcement, conventions and stereotyping. The following suggestions for teaching the topic are expressed as a series of activities, with attached comment on the ideas that should come out of these.

Play the opening of some TV genre material and discuss what comes next and how the pupils may know this – to open up the idea of shared knowledge, predictability, formula. Discuss similar material, for example in comics, and how it is that we have this knowledge of genre.

Give them a partial storyline or treatment of a TV soap episode, and ask them to complete it. This will deal with anticipation, expectation, conventions, and common elements such as stock characters.

Provide a grid headed up with common genre elements and with a list of categories on the other axis, such as quiz shows, cop thrillers, computer adventure games. Ask them to describe the elements for each in the boxes. This will make the point that genre runs across media, and operates on a formula basis. Encourage discussion of variations on the formula here and elsewhere. One should not promote the idea that genre material is inherently boring or inferior. Point out that there have been fine books and films which make intelligent use of audience anticipation, and play with it.

Ask for a storyboard of a confrontation sequence (briefly described) out of a soap or a thriller. This could bring out points about economies of production which make genres commercially attractive, and about repetitions of treatment (shots, for instance) as well as content.

As an option, if it is possible to sustain the topic over a period of time, one could ask students to collect references across the media to some current and popular example of genre – at this time and in Britain this might be the soap serial, *EastEnders*. This would help make the point that knowledge of genre material, and its impact, crosses media boundaries, and raises questions of realism, in that people discuss such material as part of their life experience, fudging the fact that it is fiction.

Finally, one might ask pupils in groups to put together an episode of a soap based on their school. This should raise questions about the line between life and drama. Most importantly, if this has not been discussed before, it should raise questions about the possible effects of genre material in terms of offering role models, dealing in stereotypes, and projecting values through the narrative. For example, do soaps endorse infidelity in relationships through its frequent use in the drama, or do they condemn it clearly enough through denouements which punish the perpetrators?

Teaching strategies

Case studies

A case study is a situation described through written and graphic background material. The student is given a role within the situation and a set of tasks following from it. The role would be barely defined in terms of occupation. So the pupil should keep within the bounds of probability in terms of role behaviour, but may use their discretion in terms of detail of personality. They then have to complete these tasks within the role, within the terms of the situation, and for the given audience. Obviously, the more authentic the situation and its materials the better. The tasks too should be realistic within the terms of reference. It is normal to allow the pupil to invent appropriate necessary additional information. Case studies are used on courses and as forms of assessment under examination conditions (GCSE/GCE).

A variation on the case study may be described as the *case situation*, which is much more sketchy and is usually followed only by discussion questions used to bring out the points illustrated. In this case the communication is for the teacher.

The advantage of the case study approach is that it puts communication within a context. One may be asking the pupil to pretend to take on a role, but the papers and the tasks can be very authentic and gain credibility with students because of this. It is also a valuable teaching method because it is controllable. The teacher sets up the terms of reference in order to deal in a certain kind of background, and in order to make the pupil perform certain tasks. They can then be sure of what has been covered. The element of control also extends to being able to put these case studies in front of the individual pupil for completion in whatever time span is thought fit. This is much more difficult to achieve with more open-ended activities, and makes assessment relatively easier with the case study. This is not to value this method above all others, but simply to point out that it does give one a kind of active learning in which the teacher is sure of objectives and can work within known resources and ability levels.

Case studies can test skills in making communication, as well as intellectual skills in respect of extracting and making sense of information contained within the given materials. It is also possible to conceive of analytic tasks in role which could demand that, for example, the pupil has to evaluate the effectiveness of a leaflet. A case study is a very useful way of bridging theory and practice.

The possible disadvantage of a case study, apart from the preparatory work necessary, is that it is in the end only a piece of game playing. It cannot be the same as actually being a clerical assistant and having to write real letters. However, apart from building-in work experience, this condition of simulation is one that most teaching has to live with.

When writing a case study, it is worth bearing one or two things in mind. First, beware of relying too much on publicity materials. This limits one's subject matter and imagination. It is also the case that too often the tasks tend towards those of a publicity nature as well. There is merit in going to the trouble of creating pieces of material for oneself, which take one into areas of interpersonal and group communication, for example. It follows from this that the teacher should also start from the topic area and the tasks, and then look for appropriate material which can be bent to their objectives. Too often one starts with what looks like a wonderful piece of stimulus material, and then has to think hard about what can be done with it.

The question of role can be a vexed one. Obviously one cannot set the pupil tasks for which an intimate knowledge of some sophisticated role is essential. However, this need not be a problem, especially if the task is explained clearly with handholds to suggest how it should be tackled. We underestimate our students too often. There is much value in this paper role play – among other things it teaches the student to learn to put themselves in someone else's shoes. The alternative of always looking for roles that are within pupils' experience can be very limiting as well as condescending, particularly if the pupils' own experience is confined. Usually they rise to the occasion and the interest of the 'game'.

The question of how self-contained the case study should be is another point to consider. The classic version is self-contained – all the material is in front of the pupil. But it is also possible to assume knowledge on the part of the student if they have dealt with the topic on the course. For example, if the tasks require some knowledge of non-verbal behaviour in the role, and if this has been dealt with, then it is reasonable to expect the student to make use of this course learning.

This also makes the point that a case study can be a method of teaching information and ideas as well as a way of practising skills. One can provide a piece of material from the company training section on making oral presentations as a lead into a task that requires the draft of a presentation to be written for someone else in that company; or one can provide a treatment of a soap serial episode as a way of teaching that format, when the task is to write lists of key elements such as cast and locations/sets for the producer (this also teaches conventions).

There can also be one or two variations on the case study format. One which is favoured by RSA examiners, for example, is where the tasks appear at staging points as the situation and material is unfolded, rather than all together following the background material.

Multi-task assignments

These could be described as an extension of the case study, for real. One difference is that they are usually undertaken by a group, so there is the benefit of the group having to discuss how to deal with the materials and the tasks, and having to allot them. It is usually the case that these tasks also require group members to go and find things out – so one also has a classic example of information-gathering, processing and representation. More perhaps than with other teaching methods, it is also reasonable to think of having a short presentation at the end of what is likely to be a long period of activity. This is particularly valuable when interviews have taken place and there is no record of this experience. Of course it is also reasonable to ask students to keep a diary of what they have done, not least because this method does not require role play. So basically what one has on paper is a brief background to the activity, followed by a set of tasks which lead up to a final task of representation. For example, in the case of something concerned with using the telephone effectively, there could be work in the library, interviews with receptionists and telephone sales people, leading up to the production of a wall chart and a role-play presentation to the rest of the group.

The advantage of this approach is that it puts the onus for learning squarely on the shoulders of the pupils. It is also interesting because one might assume that at least one task takes them outside the classroom. Other advantages are to do with authentic practice of decision-making and problem-solving in a group, as well as learning something indirectly about elements such as co-operation and constructive behaviour within a group. Students like working in groups for at least some of the time.

Possible disadvantages in using these elaborate activity assignments are as follows. If individuals do not pull their weight, or a group messes around, then it is possible to waste a lot of valuable course time which cannot be recovered. So it is vital to keep checking on who is doing what, and how effectively. Ultimately, if the group fails to work together and to achieve, then it fails to complete and is judged accordingly. This is a realistic experience. But such failure is relative and is always positively instructive. It is also usually the case that some group members do some good work which can be recognized and rewarded.

Another problem arises with having several groups within a class doing the same thing. If they do, then one may have difficulty with all the groups wanting to go to some individual or source of information at the same time. So it is ideal to have a variation on one's scenario and tasks which is not so different in principle, but which spreads the load.

Thus if you want to write a multi-task assignment, think about how you will supervise it, and make sure that everyone in the groups does work. Think about how you want to rig it so that individuals actually produce something, or whether you wish to reward every outcome as a group piece in which everyone gets the same mark or grade. Try and take the point, even when working in a school with relative difficulties of pupil release, that this type of assignment is a great opportunity for requiring the pupil to go out into the community and deal with the public. Also take the point that multi-tasks often require some kind of information-gathering before the tasks can be completed. Your role as teacher will in fact be one of facilitator – checking schedules, giving help with telephone calls to set up interviews, finding the glue to help paste up the displays. Most of all you should be thinking about what package of tasks you would put together. You might choose tasks because you want some skills practised – e.g. working in graphic formats. You might choose tasks on which you think that pupils can easily work together – e.g. composing and administering a questionnaire. And of course you must think about what holds the tasks together – e.g. the feasibility of creating a local adventure playground.

Simulations

Ken Jones has written an excellent book called *Design Your Own Simulations* (London: Methuen, 1985) in which he is something of a stickler about the distinctions between simulations, role plays, and games. We would simply offer the following distinctions, not being so sure about the importance of these. One is talking about a teaching method in which the learners are asked to work within a pretended situation and to play assumed parts. The degree of realism of the situation and parts played is variable. In a simulation there should be a fair degree of plausibility about what people do and who they are meant to be. The point is to provide a close imitation of real experience so that the participants learn something about communication as it would be in that real situation. The point of a role play is the role itself, so that backgrounds are often sketchy. The point of a game is the activity, not the role or the situation. The game is designed to get people doing something that brings out ideas or skills.

One thing that all these types must have in common is that they cause people to interact, so communication takes place whether or not it is framed within a role. It is also the case that there are not actually many examples of simulations easily available, least of all in the categories of interpersonal and group communication. They are commonly used in industrial training where specific situations are known to arise, and their specific problems can be worked out through simulating the sort of thing that is known to happen. But if you want simulations, you will probably have to write them yourself.

So why bother? Well, for a start, simulations evoke real behaviours and real responses which teach the participants something about the parallel real life situation. They generate excitement. They bring out interpersonal skills. They are seen to be worthwhile not only for the obvious effort that goes into preparing and running them, but because they do feel like the real thing. In fact it is important to debrief simulations and role plays so that pupils are reminded in the end that it was not for real, and any conflicts generated do not get carried into the lunch break. There is nothing like putting together a newspaper front page to a deadline to teach something about constraints on media production. There is nothing like simulating a school governors' meeting for learning about the rules which govern communication, about effective and ineffective contribution to groups, as well as about disagreement and decision making.

The difficulties of using simulations as a method of teaching are mostly to do with the mechanics. A full-blown simulation has a number of pieces of paper, information to be absorbed and used, and a schedule of activities to be adhered to. It is hard work setting up and running such an activity over a number of class periods. Another disadvantage is that there may not be much material evidence of what has been achieved. It is possible to have a simulation in which someone has the role of note taker, or even has to write up a summary. Otherwise what is said and how it is said remains only in the minds of the participants. So the idea of video-recording or using observers (see below) is a useful one. It may be thought that a disadvantage is getting pupils to take it all seriously. In our experience this virtually never happens, and only with a few individuals. The capacity of students to produce authentic and inventive performances in simulation and role play never ceases to amaze us. One last problem concerns numbers and space. It is difficult to create a useful simulation for much more than eight or nine people. This means that you will either have to find other spaces for other groups in the class to carry on their simulations at the same time; or you will have to be prepared to have more than one going on in the same classroom; or you will have to send off quite a number from your class (case study work in the library?) so that they all get their turn on their own. What is not attractive as a solution is the goldfish bowl effect, where most of the class sit around watching tense peers risking their confidence in a piece of pretend.

So, if you are thinking of writing a simulation in which a group of pupils play out parts within a given situation, then you should include the following:

A briefing sheet for the teacher/yourself, which sketches in the purpose of, timing of and tasks for the simulation. This enables the experience to be initiated and controlled properly. It makes clear what resources may be needed. Players need to be taken through what they are meant to be doing, when and how.

Background sheets for the participants, which tell them what they are all supposed to know (as opposed to individual knowledge) and what they are supposed to do, when and with whom.

Profiles for the participants which define their roles and behaviour to a greater or lesser degree. The further outside their experience the role is, then the more they will need to know about items such as jobs, and the background to the character. Do remember to give enough time for reading and taking in profiles and background sheets. You can all discuss the background, and deal together with any problems that are thrown up. It is worth going round individual pupils to reassure them about what they have to do, and to talk through their profiles.

Background materials for any of the given tasks, such as price lists if your situation is set in a department store. Sometimes these are necessary for everyone. Sometimes they may be given to certain individuals. Sometimes they may be given out while the simulation is in progress. It can be very useful if someone produces a piece of privileged information which may suddenly help them win an argument. Or it can be very interesting to watch a group react to an urgent fax document which throws a spanner in the works of their discussion.

We have already suggested that it is useful to have observers to act as human notebooks for what has taken place. Give them specific things to look out for – perhaps the behaviour of the chair in a meeting. They may also need their own briefing sheet.

A few points which are not to do with documents . . . we have talked about taking time to set it up. Also take time to debrief it. Justify your investment of time and organization. Make sure that people have their fair say. Make the observers work for their living. And be sure that you keep the main points of the exercise in mind, so that this point can be emphasized at the end. You will also have to consider how far you want to generate conflict by setting up two sides. For example, you could have a jury situation which is all about decision-making, and you could load the profiles to create disagreement to see whether this is resolved or not. Most of all, when debriefing, make sure that participants talk about their *assumed* role behaviour, especially when there is conflict. Make sure that it is understood that this has been, ultimately, a pretence. It is important that feelings of conflict or of failure remain within the sphere of the simulation and are not carried into real life.

Short role plays

We have already explained what these are. In this case, one provides a very brief sketch of the situation and the barest instructions for activity, possibly a three- or four-line account of the character and what they should do.

One obvious point of this method of teaching is to bring out the influence of role in groups. Sketch in a situation in which there is an authority figure, and see how far the players defer to this person. It is also possible to examine the kind of non-verbal behaviour and speech adopted by people as appropriate to their roles. One can create role plays with a built-in problem, perhaps of a personal or social nature, and use them to practise and review interpersonal skills necessary for dealing with the problem. Used this way, role plays can teach strategies for communication, especially when dealing with parents, teachers, or employers, and when learning to cope with public situations.

There are two advantages in this method. One is that role plays don't take long to write, set up, or play out, but one can get a lot out of them, especially if video-recorded. The other is that they are a way of practising communication skills without the risks of real embarrassment or breakdown, which can happen when information-gathering for a multi-task, for instance. The disadvantage is that the sketchy nature of treatment sometimes causes pupils to demand more background, and become frustrated.

If you are trying to set up a short role play, then the main thing is to work out what roles you want enacted and why. The paragraph above provides some ideas as to what one might be trying to bring out. Whatever, it makes a lot of sense to use simulations and role play freely for bringing out concepts and skills in interpersonal and group communication. As with most of the methods, we would advise against overkill. Too much of anything, and one is likely to be faced with a groan of, 'oh no, not another simulation!' Also, do remember that they can be used in your media units as well.

Individual and group assignments

Everything around you and your students is potential source material for communication work. So it is essential to have some sort of coherent overall strategy into which specific topics and activities can fit. It is, however, our view that no overall strategy or scheme of work should be so rigid that issues of topical interest cannot be incorporated when this is suddenly necessary.

The essential tasks for the teacher in devising simple assignments are: first to define the ideas or skills that you wish to bring out; then to organize these into some sort of sequence; then to select appropriate source materials; then to design the whole into a practicable student activity.

Often such an activity requires analytic and problem-solving skills in the first place, followed by productive skills in creating and presenting particular material in a particular way for a particular purpose to a particular audience. Remember that this presentation could be in any one (or more) of a number of forms – written, visual, oral, graphic, and so on.

Well-conceived assignments will help; students become more responsible for their own learning, more familiar with various communication formats, more able to take a problem-solving approach, more aware of the concepts and issues behind communication tasks, and more used to working to a brief and to a deadline.

Questionnaires

These are important strategies for exercises and skills concerned with information-gathering. They may be used to collect factual information about audience type, knowledge and opinion. They can be short and general, or lengthy and specific; administered personally by the pupil, or left for filling-in and later collection. They certainly require logical thinking. They can be part of multi-task assignments. They may well involve the pupil in the useful experience of interacting with adults, as well as working outside the classroom.

They focus the mind wonderfully if approached properly. The student has to think carefully about what they need to know and what they do not know when constructing a questionnaire. They are indispensable to pre- and post-testing of a major piece of communication, as exemplified by projects. They are obviously useful as a way of showing students how one can attempt to objectify knowledge and experience. They are also particularly useful if one insists that the pupils administer them personally, because this forces them into communication on an adult basis and also provides a means of justifying an exchange which puts the student in the driving seat. So questionnaires are a method of teaching intellectual and interpersonal skills, apart from providing information on their subject matter.

When putting together questionnaires it is important to keep an eye on the following basic points. There should be an introduction explaining very briefly what it is about, who is conducting it and why, for the benefit of the audience. It is a good idea to start with simple closed questions anyway, to encourage those filling them in. One may want to proceed to graded questions in which answers are filled in around scales of preference or degrees of knowledge, for example. Then there are open questions, which often provide the most interesting responses, even if they are difficult to process. When advising on layout remember to leave enough space for answers. Finally, don't forget to require your pupils to put that all-important 'thanks for your help' at the end.

Grids

The idea of putting information or ideas into boxes may not seem exciting, nor even conducive to open-ended thinking. But remember that the students need certitudes for a while, and no ambiguity. It is very useful to use grids to organize the characteristics of various forms of communication, for example, so that one may see their similarities and differences at a glance. A grid may be used to summarize the advantages and disadvantages of using a given form of communication, or to summarize constructive and obstructive communication behaviour between people or in groups. The very limitations of the format are its advantages – it condenses points into a structure which is visible and comprehensible. When setting these grids up as a class exercise do remember to make clear your terms of reference and the kind of brief phrasing required. It may seem easy to you, but pupils are in fact learning how to select and summarize as well as how to organize knowledge and experience.

Projects

By *project* we mean a sustained piece of work over several weeks or months which requires a range of research and creative skills. In particular, this work leads to the creation of a piece of communication in some format. Such work should be as realistic as possible, meeting an actual need for an audience, and not being just a personal or academic exercise. We are not thinking of a research essay, nor of a cut-up and paste collection of material.

Having said that, we believe that the most worthwhile project work comes from a student who is really personally committed to the task. If a student is interested in, say, analysing newspapers then he or she needs to reflect on what purpose such analysis might serve, who might need it, and how it might be presented. Answers to such questions could lead to a learning package for eleven-year-olds or to a guide to achieving publicity on behalf of a pressure group. If a student is obsessed by stamp collecting then similar

How does one teach?

Figure 3.3 Model for a communication project in terms of skills

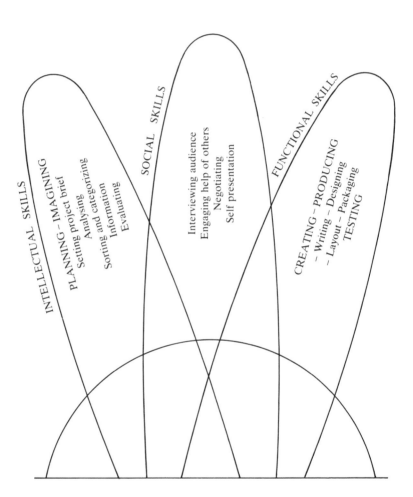

THE PROJECT

questions might lead to a communication project on ways of making a profit from stamps, or to something on stamps as works of art. However, it is worth bearing in mind that very obsessive and personal projects are prone to lapse into a self-indulgent effort. In the last case, this might produce something of interest only to committed philatelists and to the creator, something which does not engage with communication principles in its production.

So long as such traps are avoided, communication project work has many advantages. It provides opportunities for developing a range of communication skills and for applying principles of communication. The student can learn about the realistic use of resources (technologies, time, people), planning, negotiation, interviewing, research, designing and administering questionnaires, meeting deadlines, working with other people, and developing presentation skills.

Additionally, the process of completing a project is a worthwhile learning activity, almost regardless of the quality of the finished artefact. As a teacher setting up a student project you need to stress the central role of self-reflective and self-analytical approaches. The keeping of some sort of diary or log of ideas, contacts, activities, plans and failures is a crucial part of this learning process, and should form the basis of a concluding review, assessment, or commentary on the final achievements compared with the initial aims.

It is perhaps negative to talk about disadvantages to what is generally a most valuable teaching strategy, and one which is formally required by some syllabuses. But it is at least worth noting that, as with all sustained work, the biggest problem is to maintain interest, and to combat procrastination and lethargy. So it is always worth operating a regular system of checking, and having lessons in which one has a 'surgery' on progress and problems. We think it is a good idea to make students write a summary report of their achievements to date at regular intervals, so that they cannot delude themselves as to what they have achieved, and have yet to complete.

When students are embarking on such a major piece of work they often find it difficult to get started. You can help by getting them to think around ideas such as:

what are my own interests?
what contacts do I have?
what communication skills do I have or do I want to develop?
what media do I want to use?
what are my present and future career ideas?
what forms could my final piece of work take?

what needs am I aware of for any particular audience?
what audience groups do I have access to?

If these general questions reveal some potential ideas they can be refined, and planning issues raised, through questions such as:

can I describe clear aims?
can I define a specific audience grouping?
can I gain access to the necessary resources?
can I complete in the time available?
can I find ways of testing what I aim to create?
can I now make a practicable plan of action?

Some projects, for instance to make some sort of video tape, are unlikely to be completed by one person without recruiting some sort of production team. In these cases it may be desirable to form a pair or group in order to complete the work. This would usually be the way of tackling the task in the real world. But in a learning situation such long-term collaboration may lead to tension and difficulties. Also, if the teacher wants to use the project as a means of assessing individual students (see A level and GCSE in particular), then such collaboration may pose problems. There would need to be clear evidence of who had done what. It depends on the requirements of a particular course; if group work and group assessment is possible, then group projects can be a means of developing group dynamics skills as well as research and production skills.

The GCSE and A levels, at least, require the completion of a log of progress and approach, and also a commentary at the end on method and achievements which also evaluates the work. These documents are valuable in any project work, but they do require the teacher to give positive guidance and stimulus to completing them. Lessons about filling in logs, based on some key questions, are a good idea. Similarly, one should give class time for the commentary, so that the pupils learn how to complete these documents constructively at the time, rather than finding out too late what they should have done, when the work is in and assessment has to happen regardless. The syllabuses and teacher mark sheets for the A level and GCSE syllabuses provide good examples of key questions and headings for these documents.

Finally in this note on project work we want to stress a factor that is often left unstated. A sustained piece of production can enable the student not just to follow slavishly conventional formats, but to approach a task with originality and imagination. It is valuable if the teacher can encourage an original choice of format or a fresh approach within a familiar format.

Storyboards

A storyboard is, strictly speaking, a format of communication. It is a means of representing and conceptualizing a visual narrative. In film and television it is far more likely to be used in fiction than in documentary. And then it is most likely to be used for conceiving specific sequences, probably ones where action is involved. Other specific examples include titles and advertising films. A storyboard can also be used to visualize a tape slide sequence.

A storyboard is a sequence of sketched frames depicting either key shots in a longer sequence, or every single shot (and even views within elaborate shots) for a tight sequence. It may have some notes on the shot and camera work accompanying it. One would not usually expect to see anything about the sound track. Such information would usually be dealt with through a script, especially where dialogue is concerned. If it is necessary to represent sound and vision together, then you might find it useful to draw up your own sheets based on the four-part structure shown in Figure 3.4.

The advantage of a storyboard is that it forces the student to think visually, without having to be good at drawing. It is relatively unusual, and therefore stimulating. It puts the student in the position of being the creator of a visual narrative without having a camera in their hands. In this sense it is almost essential to attempt the format if one is taking on any kind of media work. It can save time and grief if used to help plan a film or video. It is an obvious and attractive exercise if one is dealing with a central topic such as advertising and persuasion.

One minor disadvantage is that one really needs to prepare sheets of blank frames, to avoid pupils wasting time drawing them. Otherwise, there is not a great deal for the teacher to do. It is useful to reassure pupils that stick drawings and written instructions are an acceptable way of representing their vision. It is important that they are prepared to conceive various shots, camera movements, and shifts in narrative. It is useful to give out sheets of drawings for these and the storyboard, so that they can see by example.

Content analysis

This is an objective approach to communication material in which one tries to quantify what is evident, as well as to classify it. Usually the method is applied to media material. One may analyse techniques and method as well as subject matter and content. In the case of a magazine, for instance, one could express the proportion of advertisements as a percentage of the total number of pages, or do the

Figure 3.4 Specimen standard script sheet for film, video, slide-tape

Time	Sound	Visuals	No.

same for illustrations. It is reasonable to apply the same principle of careful counting to, for example, the number of pictures in a women's magazine in which the subject is looking out of the frame, or the number of head shots used in a soap serial. In all cases, it comes down to the fact that if there is a pattern, if there is a significant proportion of given items, then one may begin to make inferences about, for example, the real intentions of the producers of the communication. So it is a way of identifying covert messages, and of being able to argue that they do exist.

The advantage of the approach is that it enables pupils to engage with attractive material in a systematic manner. It requires them to pay close attention to their subject matter, and forces them to notice patterns and correlations which they might otherwise miss. It enables them to find things out for themselves. The disadvantage can be that, regardless of one's chivvying, pupils do like to read and chat about the material as opposed to scan, select and discuss. A problem, rather than a disadvantage, can be that pupils tend to feel that they have done everything if they have described and presented carefully, and may need chivvying to move on to levels of interpretation.

As an activity it recommends itself to a pair or small group approach. It also lends itself to graphic representation of the figures obtained, quite possibly for class display and discussion. In terms of writing the task sheets, one needs to give some hints about what to look for in the type of material being studied. In terms of conducting the activity, do set deadlines and keep checking progress. Encourage students to cut out typical examples for illustration.

What can you do with a magazine?

There is a tendency to think that the study of communication and mass media requires considerable investment in hardware and software. Of course, if you can manage individual access to cassette recorders, video cameras and playback machines and editing suites, as well as to personal computers, then obviously you and your students are well-placed to develop a range of technology-based communication skills and concepts.

However, it is our view that you can achieve a lot of intellectual, social and functional communication competence with everyday cheap materials. For instance, magazines are throwaway goods that you can easily accumulate free from pupils, students, friends and colleagues. They can provide a recurring source of activity at several levels. In this section we simply want to point to some of the ways in which you could use magazines for communication work – and we hope that these suggestions will serve to stimulate further tactics from you.

How often does your group ask, 'What are you doing this for?' This may well arise if you suggest a group begin to bring magazines (or even more, comics) into classroom. We believe magazines can provide a stimulus for developing techniques of observing, analysing, comparing, discussing, and presenting in imaginative and factual ways: all of which are useful life and work skills. Naturally, any of your pupils who aim to make careers in journalism and the media, as many do, will find magazine work intrinsically interesting. In addition to developing the skills suggested above, we also consider that this work can contribute to a conceptual grasp of communication principles as well as economic, social and moral issues.

Magazine activities

Brain-storming on the question 'What can you use a magazine for?' Getting individuals, then pairs, then groups, to be as imaginative as possible is worth doing regularly. In brain-storming ideas should not be criticized or filtered out at first; everything should be listed. Can the group fill a side of paper with things to do? If the two aspects of (i) obtaining different sorts of information in words and pictures and (ii) using the physical object for various purposes are listed from all sorts of perspectives, then we may have some sort of idea why we spend millions per year on thousands of magazines.

Observing what magazines are available Discovering the range of magazines available by shop and library research often surprises people. Let them check the numbers and titles of publications that are listed in a reference book such as *Willings Press Guide* which is published annually. Obtain some specialist trade magazines, company house journals, or fanzines.

Comparing the variety of topics and conventions A comparison of covers, use of pictures, use of language and tone, layout, colour, size, price, publishers, topics, advertisements and so on indicates very forcibly that the aims of a magazine, the writer/reader relationship, and the 'world-view' adopted can be infinitely varied.
  If possible get some old magazines and introduce an historical perspective. The changes in style, especially of the visuals, are remarkable and often amusing. Many magazines, particularly in their advertisements, provide a mirror of ourselves, the readers – or do they?

Analysing specific articles, pictures and advertisements The levels at which you can do this will depend on the groups. At the end of this section we have reproduced a specimen individual assignment which has been used with post-GCSE students in order to get them to make a detailed analysis of one magazine and to present their findings to the group. Alternative strategies might be to analyse a collection of similar magazines, e.g. teenage, women's, trade, leisure, or music. In presenting the results, it can be factual or it could be simply describing the typical reader as deduced from the magazine. Who does the editor think she/he is talking to?

Conducting market research One interesting way of answering that last question and at the same time gaining some insight into market research and economics of a magazine is to obtain some marketing manuals from magazines which they use for advertisers. Most magazines are selling magazines to readers and selling readers to advertisers, hence magazine publishers need to state who their readers are for the benefit of potential advertisers.

Magazine reading can give a worthwhile focus for some pupil surveys using questionnaires and interviews to explore the general themes of 'what magazines do you read and why do you read them?'

Applying models and concepts of communication Again the depth of this will depend on the group, but it is possible to use magazine analysis to illustrate three key models: First, the process model incorporating aims, messages, media, intended audience and effects. Second, the semiotic model of engaging with a 'text' and unpeeling the layers of personal, cultural and economic meanings. Third, the mass media 'uses and gratifications' model. These are not the only conceptual approaches, of course.

Producing your own magazine This lends itself well to a group project and can apply the foregoing analytical processes: identifying need, audience, topics, preparing text and visuals, creating advertisements, techniques of printing, and so on to make it as real as possible.

Communication studies assignment: magazine analysis and report

Choose a magazine or journal: I suggest not one you usually read or a 'Sunday supplement'.

A   Analyse the magazine as follows:
1   Factual details, e.g. size, length, price, format, publisher
2   Visual impact, including the cover
3   Topics covered
4   Products and services advertised

5 Proportion of editorial topics and advertisements
6 Analyse one article/story for content, style, etc.
7 Analyse two advertisements for content, style, visuals, persuasive techniques
8 What do you consider to be target audiences?
9 What do you think of the magazine? Give your opinions.

B Present your findings as a report with the usual headings, graphic presentation, etc.

C Prepare notes and at least one overhead projector transparency for a four-minute presentation to a group of communications students.

Deadline: Completed by

Teaching and using technology

This section provides some ideas as to how one uses video, audio, photography, and word-processing in a course. This may be with the intention of providing basic familiarity with the technology, but it may also be used as a means of learning concepts and skills. In general, we offer the proviso that it is perfectly possible to teach productively without this technology. On the other hand, if you have access to some of it, then it may be helpful to have a few ideas as to what to do with it. In no way are we trying to provide a handbook to the mechanics of using, say, a video camcorder. All we would say is that usually it is a lot easier than it looks from the handbooks provided by manufacturers. We suggest that two or three hours spent using the equipment yourself will enable you to summarize do's and don'ts for your pupils on two or three sides of A4. Fear not!

Replay and video in the classroom

There are limits to what one can discuss here because there are copyright limits to what one is allowed to use, if we are talking about off-air material. Suffice to say that there is something curious and unhealthy about a society which cannot allow most of its broadcast communication to be used in the classroom. The values of ownership and profit appear to prevail over those of education.

With the material that you can use, there is probably one major rule of methodology. In most cases don't play complete programmes or films. Ignore the groans when the narrative is interrupted. It is there to be unlocked and used as a tool, not to be a repeat of that illusory seamless viewing experience at home or in the cinema. Use the pause for examination of a frame or sequence. Use it to review segments of tape and to demand answers to questions. Be prepared to search back and replay in order to settle an argument.

Always preview and cue tapes against the counter if you possibly can. Otherwise you will waste embarrassing minutes searching material. It looks good to be able to punch the button on your own verbal cue, or to be able to shuttle through numbers in a few seconds and then say 'now look at this'. Preparation enables one to move from tape to tape or item to item quickly, drawing together examples, and making points about the repetition of material.

Replayed video offers an enormously rich vein of source material, not just for teaching about the media. One obvious use is to look at conversational exchanges, at strategies in action, at self-presentation, and at non-verbal behaviour. Slow-motion facilities on the video enable one to look in detail at what is happening, or one can repeat sequences to bring out points. Bearing in mind that one might have to ask for this to be done at home, consider the following examples of viewing to cover the above: chat shows for conversation, interviews with politicians for strategies, quiz show hosts for self-presentation, and situation comedies for non-verbal behaviour. This is all communication in action.

Of course, television is an object of study in its own right. The whole business of genres, conventions and stereotypes is the bulk of much of television's output. These can only be understood and discussed by looking at the material itself, even if this has to happen at home under teacher guidance.

In particular, students need to be able to see and hear the devices of sound and picture, to spot shot changes, to see how editing works. Video controls the flow and exposes the artifice. Pupils can see how television advertisements are put together effectively, and of course can practise their own through storyboarding. It is possible to embark on shot-by-shot breakdowns, and to discuss why and how they are used (just as it is possible to analyse conversation in the same way and see the individual signs of non-verbal communication).

Video cameras and recording

Then there is the question of video as a tool. Whereas replay is available in some form to all schools and colleges, camera recording is a different matter, with camcorders costing a thousand pounds each. But if you can get one, use it, but preferably not to try and make your own programmes or films in the first place. Exciting as this is, it is also time-consuming, and probably beyond the resources of many. In the first place, use the machine as a recording medium. Use it to record simulations, role plays, classroom activities. Use it to record interviews. The sense of using the medium creatively and constructively could come out of these activities if there is time. As a method of teaching, class recorded video is invaluable for teaching pupils how to make effective presentations, and for showing them how they did or did not solve a problem in a group.

If you are lucky enough to have video editing facilities, then do remember that an edit suite is useful for simply assembling material for replay in the classroom. One can put together the best bits of role plays for use with classes. Obviously you have the ability to put together documentary pieces or short pieces of drama, but remember that it is also possible to edit in the camera if you prepare work carefully, and know exactly what shots will follow each other. This kind of preparation is necessary even if you have an edit suite (though of course this does enable you to cover mistakes!). Edit in camera simply means that these machines will replay your sequence of shots as recorded without a jump on screen between each shot. However, we will go on assuming that you only have access to the camera (probably a camcorder, which is an all-in-one camera/recorder/replayer).

If you do want to use video for its own sake, then we would suggest the following basic rules and activities for working with students. If you or a student are recording classroom activity, then take account of the following. We assume that you will want to work off batteries, and not be tied to a mains lead. Before filming check your batteries for charge; check that you have set the lens so that most objects will be in focus most of the time; practise shots if necessary; check that your tape is in and will run; check that you have pressed a button for white balance (colour range); make sure that you have switched off any figure displays seen in the view-finder. Also set the indoor/outdoor button – if there is any daylight, use the outdoor setting, even if you have lights on. Set the focus on manual (not auto), because most autos are rather slow and inconvenient.

During filming, a tripod or firm surface is excellent for producing steady shots, though it does make it difficult to move around easily and to change point of view (POV). Handheld on the shoulder works very well with a little practice precisely because one can vary POV, angle, etc. It is desirable to provide this variation, making sure one has both sides of a conversation, by standing on a chair, crouching down, etc. Remember that one can pause the recording between each shot change. You may miss a little bit of the action, but this editing in camera makes the replay look so much better on screen. Of course you will want to vary closeups and general shots, and be prepared to hold a closeup on a face if you are looking for expressions, or wanting to listen to what is being said. In general, don't use much zoom/pulling in tight: it is disturbing to view. Don't aim at lights, windows, sky – you will get a lot of light and no picture. Avoid moving the camera too much during a shot. What you might call 'looking around' becomes a dizzy blur on screen.

With regard to sound, simply remember that the built-in microphones are limited, and pick up the loudest sound, including the lawnmower outside the window. You may have to lose clarity of sound some of the time. When you want to hear conversation, then try to work within ten feet of the subject. There are options such as attaching an external microphone and getting someone else to hold it in the right place, but you need to practise this.

One or two other points – it is useful to 'mark' your recording by speaking into the mike at the beginning of the recording, saying who, what and when. It is even possible to write a caption card and record this quickly. These machines have fade in and fade out buttons which make the beginning and end look more professional if used. You can also try tricks for linking segments (especially if you pause for a while), such as zooming into someone's back, then cut, then zoom out from someone else's back from another point of view. One thing, if you put the machine on pause for too long it will eventually jump out to a standby mode (or even switch off if it is an old model): it is worth checking what happens in these circumstances, because older models may disengage the tape so that when you start recording again they record over the last few seconds of your last shot.

If you are recording outside then really the same points apply, but remember that it is even harder to get clean sound, and more likely that you will pick up traffic or wind noise. So get in really close in *vox pops* (street interviews). Watch out for distracting action in the background, such as small children and fighting dogs.

If you are trying to make a more elaborate piece of organized drama, then the same points are still relevant. It is simply vital to practise shots, to have a script, to have rehearsed action, and to get used to the idea of asking people to repeat action for you to record it from different angles. It is also essential to keep a log of every shot, otherwise you will never sort out which shot is which. In this case, and if you know that you are going to edit it, leave a gap between each take.

If you have an edit suite then you can do clever things like re-record conversation and put in on the tape. But even without, you can use audio dub facilities to do things like put on some narration or put on some music. If you have the time, have a go. You have nothing to lose. You cannot harm the machinery. At the end of it all, the great thing about video is that the tape is re-usable (though for recording and re-use it is worth buying quality tape such as Scotch).

Finally, if you do want to teach use of video in a more formal sense, then we would recommend that you should structure the sessions, with advice and task sheets, so that the students have specific goals but can also manage on their own for much of the time. One possible sequence of activities is as follows. Start with hands-on explanation, but briefly. Then let them shoot wild for about ten minutes and review. This will get impatience and silly mistakes out of the way. Then ask them to record a short interview to camera. Then a conversation, with variation of POV. Then prepare a brief documentary or story piece, including all the shots, and shoot it in sequence, to edit in camera. Short units of activity, with the promise of rapid replay (the best part!), keep students involved. But also remember that only one person can handle the camera at a time, so, unless you can borrow more cameras, you need to organize your classes into small groups, with various activities to keep them occupied.

Information technology: word-processing

Unless you are working in a college, and probably with vocational courses, you are unlikely to get hold of enough machines to teach much of a hands-on nature to a whole class. There is a degree of mist and fog surrounding the teaching of new technology, particularly in the practical sense. There are even some false claims made about what is actually being achieved. It is important if at all possible to teach something about the various applications of new technology, and about the implications of its presence for work and leisure. There are some fair video tapes around to act as a starting point for explanation and discussion, for example the series available via *Sunday Times* publications (*Computing and Your Business* (1989), Taylor Made Distributors, Harrington Dock, Liverpool X, L70 1AX).

But when it comes to using machines, apart from sheer availability, one also has to consider why one wants to spend course time on this anyway. Most communication students do not need to use databases to store and sort information, or spread sheets to arrange and process financial information. They would find it interesting to see how mail systems and information networks operate – TTNS is the educational version. But it is not the end of the world if they do not have this experience, in spite of large statements made about computer literacy. In terms of micro computers (very likely the ubiquitous BBC) they might profit from various language programmes, if they need to enhance basic linguistic skills. They would also gain from using a desk top publishing programme such as *AMX Pagemaker* to practise newspaper and magazine layout.

But most of all they would benefit from being able to use a word processor. Apart from being able to lay out text, and play with elements such as type face, it enables one to produce clean corrected text. This text is being produced initially by two fingers and an Amstrad word processor. These machines can be a boon to those of us with poor handwriting. They can also help those with spelling difficulties. We do not advocate them as a substitute for trying to handwrite and spell effectively – public examinations demand this. But the fact is that these machines are quite cheap and easy to learn to use.

There are many word-processing programmes available for various microcomputers. Nevertheless you will go a long way to beat the *Locoscript 2* programme used on Amstrad machines made for the purpose. The basic 8256 model is cheaper than many electronic typewriters and will do a lot more, including running other kinds of programme referred to above. If you are using one of the ubiquitous BBC machines, then there are at least three useful processing packages about: *Interword*, *Wordwise Plus*, and *View*. The last two are available on a ROM chip that is bought as a feature of the machine. Of these *Wordwise* is very friendly but somewhat limited. *View* is probably the most accessible and useful. Ideally, everyone should learn to touch type, in order to learn to use keyboards fast. But, given the fact that one can correct mistakes easily, this is not essential. A word processor enables students to produce clean copy for projects, fair simulations of documents such as a press release and magazine pages (especially if one uses some cut-and-paste of printouts and then photocopies). For some it brings competence and imagination out into the light of day.

There are a number of sound handbooks with exercises for these basic programmes. If you cannot afford some of these, then it is still not that hard to produce some handhold sheets of your own – on the word processor. In terms of use and possibly some practical sessions, as with video, it is possible to make pupils largely independent in learning.

The first thing they need to know is how to load the programme and get the screen ready to use. Then they need to have a reference or tutored guidance on the main key functions, but there is no great mystique about this. Very few key strokes are needed to turn text into italics, emboldened, in small letters, and with a justified right hand margin. Then they need to know how to save what is on screen on to the disc and how to print it out.

Once they can actually use the machine, then it is, again, a good idea to put them through a few specific exercises. Try a few which require using key functions to change the look of the text. Ask them to compose a letter of application for a specific job. Ask them to write up their own CV under given headings (and of course keep it for later adaptation). Ask them to lay out some text for a sheet of a leaflet.

What you will find is that at least some pupils will want to spend all their spare time in front of the machine. You will find that it is vital to label discs and their contents carefully. Probably it is best to have a rule that only you may wipe items from discs. You will need to husband your printer ribbons. One way of doing this is to teach students to print in single strike for most drafts of documents, and save the good double strike for final copies. You can also keep worn ribbons for general use, and save a good ribbon for insertion when there is fair copy to be printed. Finally, make it a rule that no one takes drinks within five feet of the machine.

Making audio tapes

Producers of broadcast-quality sound tapes still use reel-to-reel recorders and edit by splicing the tape. They also have access to studios with facilities for mixing and editing. In this section we are not expecting or advocating this level of technology, although if you can get access to it you will obviously be able to achieve better results technically.

We start rather from the basis that you and your students are likely to have easy access to some cassette tape recorders with built-in microphones. As with video cameras, it is worthwhile using external microphones, which are fairly cheap. Similarly, a basic sound-mixing unit for dubbing can be bought quite cheaply. However, if you simply want voice over music or other sound source, you can play the sound source tape on one machine whilst speaking over it and recording both on to a second machine: you may need a few run-throughs to get the levels acceptable.

Even just with two simple cassette recorders individual students or small groups can have fun, learn about how radio as a medium works, and develop a range of communication skills, such as planning, audience defining, researching, selecting, formulating aims, scripting, revising, speaking, performing, and working as a team. The attractions of 'radio production' are that it is cheap and provides scope for imaginative work: some of the productions we have listened to have been technically sub-standard because of inadequate equipment, but conceptually exciting because of the creativity shown by the students (some have also been self-indulgent rubbish of interest to no one but the makers).

There are a variety of formats and genres that can be used. First, sound tapes can simply be used as a record, for example of interviews, conversations, discussions, role plays or any sort of group work. We would stress interviews in particular because the others are more effective on video. The practice of formulating questions and answers within clearly-defined aims and contexts is worthwhile and can be caught well on sound tape. Indeed, interviewing techniques are a basic skill that can then be developed to produce 'programmes'.

News tapes can be recorded from local or national newspapers (with the necessary selecting and rewriting for listening), or from school/college events with reports and interviews, which will require careful scripting for time limits, and careful use of words and linguistic structure for clarity according to the target audience. Your students may not have compared news broadcasts from local commercial and BBC radio, or from BBC Radio 1 and Radio 4 – the selection and presentation of the same day's news may be quite different.

Creating sound advertisements can also be challenging. The mix of music, sounds, voices and 'drama' for real or imaginary products or services in thirty seconds or one minute forces a tight discipline. Students can simulate real broadcast advertisements or deliberately break the conventions and stereotypes.

Depending on the time available, students can be encouraged to develop tapes at more length, with documentary treatment of a topic such as the local area, a local issue, or a favourite place or person. Improvising and/or scripting a piece of sound drama is also feasible. Alternatively, an instructional tape could be produced – how to prepare a meal, repair a puncture, use a word processor . . .

BBC Radio Bristol has produced a pack of material for students on how to make a radio tape, which as well as practical advice includes jargon to impress your friends. Other local radio stations may produce similar materials or may have a community or education liaison person ready to help you and your students.

Slide-tape production

Producing slide-tape sequences is well within the technical possibilities of any school or college. All you need is a slide projector and a cassette recorder. Professional slide-tape productions using several synchronized projectors, stereo sound and maybe multiple screens are not what we have in mind in this section. A book such as *Effective Audio-visual: A User's Handbook* by Robert Simpson (London: Focal Press, 1987) provides information on the use of professional productions. The opportunity to experience these is now available at many tourist spots such as historical sites and of course at marketing and PR exhibitions.

For our purposes, one projector with manually-changed slides and one cassette recorder are sufficient to give students knowledge of the principles of audio-visual presentation and the skills to create it. Also two projectors can be faded in and out without a 'dissolve unit' simply by placing the projectors side by side with manual changing and fading from one to the other with a piece of cardboard. It is possible to create automatic synchronized presentations with a single sound and slide projector, such as that produced by Bell & Howell costing a few hundred pounds.

Creating slide-tape sequences requires the same knowledge and skills as for creating sound tapes (see previous section), but also depends on using cameras or having access to slides. Ideally students will be able to produce their own slides, thus developing their camera skills; but it is possible to use ready-made slide collections in the school or to develop a collection of local places, magazine advertisements, paintings, holiday slides, etc. Slides can also be made of graphic materials and text; you can draw on slides.

Selection of visuals, audience conceptualizing, formulation of aims, researching, scripting, use of sounds and music, devising storyboards, as well as putting it all together, are all worthwhile communication work. Simply preparing a storyboard can be worthwhile since planning and conceptualizing a complete audio-visual presentation is a difficult problem-solving exercise.

Such a presentation can serve several purposes: as an art-form around your locality in images and music to stimulate favourable or unfavourable impressions; as an informative piece around your school or course or club for potential customers; as a documentary around a building, person or event; as publicity for a place to visit; or as an education package around a topic such as advertising or painting.

Since students are not usually familiar with slide-tape conventions, they can approach set tasks with fresh ideas about how to use these media to present a topic using sound and still images. One of the authors will never forget the intellectual and emotional impact of one student's slide-tape sequence on 'Animal Rights' using her own slides, slides from various associations and slides from brochures –

the intensity of seeing the abuse of animals from a series of perspectives was numbing. Slide-tape sequences may seem second-best to
video, but they can be a powerful medium.

There are several books available on the techniques of slide tape
production for more advanced presentations, for example
Slide/Sound and Filmstrip Production by John Sunier (London: Focal
Press, 1981). Focal Press publish a series of practical guides to
audio visual productions from scripting to video production. For
further details contact Focal Press Ltd., 31 Fitzroy Square, London
W1P 6BH.

Chapter four

Teaching materials

Introduction

This section of the book contains examples of materials used by the authors, which cover the range of topics referred to in Chapters 2 and 3. These samples cover:

- the possible beginning to a course (items 1, 2 and Figure 4.1).
- interpersonal, group and mass media categories (items 5, 6, 8, 9, 10, 11, 13).
- design and graphic tasks (items 3, 9, 12, 14).
- various teaching methods/types of activity (items 2, 4, 5, 6, 8, 9, 13).
- some criteria by which to measure examples and students' own work (items 3, 12).

For practical reasons, we have not included a great deal of visual material. But there should be enough across the range of content and method to provide a sound idea of our intentions and practice as described in the rest of the book.

1 Communication process – introductory exercises

The task for these exercises is to discuss the situations described in terms of how communication might be used. In particular, you should deal with the following: what forms of communication might be used; how you would describe the uses of communication in each case; and what aspects of process you might identify. You should talk about how these aspects of communication relate to how communication is carried on in each case. These aspects would include the nature of the source and of the destination of the communication; the context in which it takes place; the possibility and use of feedback; the nature of the form or medium of communication used; the message to be communicated. You are of course also concerned with how one may put across meaning through communication.

Figure 4.1 Pre-course questionnaire – Communication Studies A Level

Name ....

1   Why have you chosen to take this course?

2   What aspects of the course particularly interest you?

3   What are some of the things you expect to learn in this course?

4   What parts of the course will be the most difficult for you?

5   From your past experience rate these teaching methods :

	Very helpful	Helpful	Not productive
Class discussions			
Class lectures			
Reading on your own			
Writing essays			
Preparing for a test			
Individual or small group tutorials			
Practical work			
Working on a project individually			
Working on a project in a team			
Solving problems			
Others			

6   List the subjects you have taken at GCSE with grades and say which subjects you found the most stimulating

1. You are members of an exploration party mapping the highlands of New Guinea in the East Indies. You come across a group of tribesmen whose language you do not speak. They are armed with wooden spears and stone axes. They look threatening but at the same time are obviously as nervous of you as you may be of them. How can you reassure them and make friendly contact?

2. You are members of a special police unit set up to go and talk to children in primary school about the dangers of contact with strangers. How should you best approach the subject and the children?

3. You are working for the local council's publicity unit. You have been given a brief to inform the public about a new road scheme to which there has already been opposition. The scheme will ease traffic problems, but it will also take away part of a park, and will also mean that some houses will have to be demolished. How could you best promote the advantages of the scheme and deal with objections?

2 Communication problems for discussion

Read the following accounts of situations in which communication becomes a problem in some way. Discuss the nature of the problem in small groups. Produce solutions to the problems. Also be ready to explain what the situations tell us about how and why communication happens.

1. Two young people, one English, one Japanese, are part of an exchange scheme linking England with Japan. The Japanese student, who speaks quite good English, has arrived to stay with the English family. For various practical reasons this visit is taking place for a month over Christmas. It is just before Christmas. The young English person is trying to explain what English people do at Christmas time and why . . .

2. A group of journalists is trying to establish a weekly newspaper in a city, as an alternative to the regional daily paper which is owned by the Westminster Press, a large publishing group. They want the newspaper to concentrate on local and community issues, and where reasonable to be more critical of local government than the regional paper. They are using new technology to publish their paper, hoping to keep the costs down. They are trying to make it attractive to the local people, and not too serious. They are happy to accept advertising if they can get it. But they seem to be having trouble in getting

through to their readership because circulation is not good . . .

3. A group of people working in the same company often go out to lunch together, and all get on well with each other. One of the group, a young woman, has been out for the evening a couple of times with one of her male colleagues. Now he is persistently asking her to continue going out. She is not that interested and is trying to work out how to get him to understand this . . .

3 General criteria by which to judge communication

These criteria also serve to further define the two key terms – appropriateness and effectiveness – frequently quoted themselves as the main criteria by which any piece of communication should be judged.

AUDIENCE: Does the communication recognize the characteristics of and needs of the audience through content, treatment and presentation in particular?

MEDIUM: Is the medium/form/format chosen for a good reason, that is having regard for the other criteria?

PURPOSE: Does the communication at least imply a sense of purpose in the selection and construction of the message?

CONTEXT: Is the effect of social and physical context taken into account, with regard to message and medium in particular?

SOURCE/SENDER: Is the communicator clear about her/his role (real or simulated), and its likely effect on the communication?

MESSAGE CONTENT: Is the substance of the communication (fact or opinion or even creative imagination) properly evident, and relevant to purpose in particular?

MESSAGE TREATMENT: Has the communicator inflected the message (in its given code or medium) with a sense of style, of the uses of communication (e.g. persuasive), with regard to purpose and audience need in particular?

CONVENTIONS: Does the use of the medium/form/format take account of accepted conventions (especially those of layout and structure), where these exist and are relevant?

These criteria are all equally important, though recognition of audience is often crucial in assessing effectiveness.

4 Short case study

Pay close attention to the notions of *audience* and *purpose*.

You work in the administrative section of a large company. There has been a problem with the air-conditioning system in the company headquarters building, and it is your responsibility to deal with some relevant paperwork. In the first place, there has been a breakdown of a component operating the louvre mechanism in an air duct. It turns out that this has been out of action for three weeks, and that in spite of verbal complaints from staff affected, the maintenance staff have done nothing about it. The effect of this breakdown has been to make one floor of the building uncomfortably warm at certain times of the day. The maintenance supervisor claims that he has not received any proper notification of the problem on the relevant form. He also says that the ventilation system should not have broken down at all as it was only installed fifteen months ago, and there is a separate maintenance contract with the suppliers to check the system once a year.

Tasks

1. Write a letter to the suppliers criticizing them for the fact that there has been such a breakdown, and questioning the fact that nothing was discovered during the first yearly check on the system.

2. Compose a memorandum to the maintenance supervisor, questioning the fact that he did not follow up verbal requests in any way, and advising a policy for future action.

3. Design a notice to go on staff bulletin boards which informs them of the need to follow correct procedures immediately when informing the relevant people about breakdowns and defects in equipment.

5 Case situations – interpersonal communication at work

You should discuss these situations with reference to those factors which would affect how interpersonal communication is carried on; and effective and ineffective ways of using communication to resolve the situations.

Situation 1 – the late employee

As a supervisor working for an overall manufacturing company, you have to deal with an employee who turns up late for her shift for the third day running. She says that she has domestic problems concerned with one of her children who has been sick. In spite of this, you feel that you cannot ignore this lateness, and must say more to her . . .

Situation 2 – the lost files

You are a newly-employed clerical assistant working in a local government department. Your immediate superior is a Deputy Principal Officer. She is giving you a hard time because she claims that you have not put a set of files on her desk. But you are sure that you put them out two days previously and that she has simply mislaid them – not for the first time. She has made such an issue of it that you feel you want to say something . . .

Situation 3 – a wrong booking

You are a receptionist working in a large hotel and you deal with bookings. You are facing an irritated client who insists that he booked a double room, but has been allocated a single one on the lists that you have. As it happens, it was a colleague of yours who actually took the booking and recorded it on the computer as being for a single room. The colleague has never made a mistake like this before, so you are inclined to think that it is the client who is at fault. However, the colleague is not around to ask, the client is in front of you, and you have to say something . . .

6 Interpersonal communication – role play

Take any of the situations described below and talk them through in terms of what may affect how communication takes place. You may wish to discuss the situations in terms of communication factors. Then try role-playing each situation, to see how things work out in practice. You may wish to discuss how you could have used communication more effectively and positively to produce a different outcome.

Role play 1 – the parking ticket

A traffic warden in a city centre area has just written out a parking ticket and fixed it to the car when the owner returns. The owner is not very happy about collecting a fine. She has just made a trip to the tax office to try and sort out a mistake on her tax code, having found nowhere else to park in time to make the appointment.

Role play 2 – the best friend

This situation involves a girl and her best friend. The friend has started going out with a man who is five years older than her, and who is rather too smooth for the first girl's liking. The girl isn't happy that her friend spends less time with her than she used to. But now, to cap it all, the girl has met someone whom she knows to be pretty honest, and who tells her that the man is not all he seems. Apparently he is known to be a petty car thief – though he hasn't actually been caught yet. So the first girl decides to go and see her best friend and have a talk with her . . .

Role play 3 – late home

In this case a young person has had to assume responsibility for looking after a fourteen-year-old sister, while mother goes into hospital for a minor operation. Father can only do so much because he is a travelling salesperson, and is away for most of the week. Everything goes well for three days, and mother has her operation. But then one evening, just when the two of you are going to see your mother in hospital, something happens. A boy friend turns up with a ticket for a concert, and says that he asked the sister out to it. But then, apart from anything else, it becomes clear that even if you do let your sister go she won't be able to get the last bus home. The boy is willing to walk her home, but the journey is one-and-a-half miles. A conversation follows . . .

7 A short case study: *The US Dollar*

A relative of yours has taken a franchise with a new US fast food chain operator known as *The US Dollar*. The franchise offers financial help with renting suitable commercial premises to company standards, as well as providing standard items of decor, standard recipes, and some food wholesale. The idea is that the financial investment and risk is spread between the franchiser and the franchisee. Both stand to make a good profit. Your relative has signed up for the franchise and has nearly completed work fitting out premises near the centre of Bristol.

The original concept of this fast food chain was to provide a snack (or a sandwich) for a dollar (about 70p). The franchising company still provides a few such lines to maintain this image, but most meals now cost between £1.00 and £2.00. What the customer is mainly offered is a choice of so-called regional dishes from the USA. For example, there is tortilla from New Mexico; Virginian potato pie; Georgia fatback bacon and peas with french fries; Kansas corn-on-the-cob; and even Capone's own recipe spaghetti from Chicago.

All this is a device to make cheap food of reliable quality attractive to customers. The franchisee can choose from a range of 'dishes' on offer, deciding what they think will sell well in their area. The operation is pitched at young singles and couples. It tries to capitalize on the glamour of US culture in its decor – for example with items like photos of rodeos, drive-ins, and so on.

Franchises, like this one, are located near the centres of towns, preferably at the edge of an identifiable leisure and entertainment area. They do lots of business midday, early and late evening, and weekends. Franchisees are bound by agreement to keep up *Dollar Company* standards. They are inspected to make sure that their operations are clean, efficient and welcoming. The company requires strict house rules for behaviour, so that their outlets are known as reliable, safe, and fair value for money (in order to attract approval from parents of at least some of the young clients).

As a gimmick in the opening month (and at later times to boost business), the company gives the franchisee a supply of silver dollars to give to anyone who brings in a party of six or more people to eat there.

Task

Design an A5-size fly sheet to publicize the opening of the Bristol *US Dollar Food Bar*. This may be designed to be folded or flat. You can't use more than two colours. This flyer would be given out in town to passers-by or would be put under car windscreen wipers. You may use your imagination to invent appropriate further details.

8 Simulation exercise: Eardleigh Health Centre

Controller's notes

This is a straightforward short simulation in which the task is basically to discuss what should be done about the proposal to put community money towards the building of a new health centre. You should be prepared to answer questions in the preliminary session, in which participants will read the background and their profiles (seen only by themselves). General questions about the place and the issues can be answered in a group, with you inventing what you may. Particular questions about profile background and attitudes should be discussed only with the relevant participant.

You will need to make it clear as to when the simulation starts and finishes. You may want to insist that only a certain time is allowed for social introductions before the serious discussion gets underway. The situation has deliberately been set up as one in which an open meeting has been called, and no one person has been delegated to run the session formally. Part of the point is to see how the 'local people' decide to organize themselves as a group. Otherwise, this is an exercise in seeing how people negotiate points of view, may or may not compromise, and are capable of reaching agreements. In all this the use of verbal and non-verbal communication is central. These are all things that should be discussed in the debriefing session. It is always important to make notes on how communication was used, especially if the debriefing must take place in sessions separate from the actual simulation.

The simulation could fall into the following pattern: fifteen minutes giving out and reading the materials; fifteen minutes answering questions collectively or individually; up to forty minutes spent on the simulation activity; up to thirty minutes spent reviewing who used communication to what effect and why: and what agreements were reached and why.

Task notes for participants

This is a simulation of a community meeting. It is set in a place and based on issues described in the background sheet. You should read this carefully, and ask the controller any questions about facts which you feel are unclear. You may also make up facts about the place and about yourselves, which you think are consistent with what you have been told.

Your task is to walk into the simulation area as directed by your controller, and start the meeting in any way that you think fit. This is an informal meeting: you may organize it in any way that you wish. Because of this and because you are not necessarily people who know one another, you are quite free to make social introductions and to exchange information about yourselves.

However, it would not make sense to talk too freely in the first place about your attitudes to the issues surrounding the proposed health centre. These you will reveal when you all get down to serious discussion about the main topic. At the end of the simulation you will have to report back to the controller and say what you have or have not agreed.

Background information

Eardleigh is a large suburb of Knighton. It still retains its old village centre of a church, two pubs and some eighteenth-century housing, but mostly it consists of more modern housing developments, some private, some council-built, with some of these council houses having been bought back by the tenants. Eardleigh has developed beyond its facilities, not least in terms of shops and of medical and social services. The view of the Local Authority is that people should travel into Knighton for whatever they need. But the bus service is notoriously poor, and there are many married women trapped in Eardleigh, as well as an increasing number of the elderly and infirm.

There is a Community Council which is supposed to represent the Eardleigh residents. It is recognized by Knighton Authority because it is in effect the old parish council of Eardleigh. It is consulted over developments, and has a small grant for running the Community Hall and its activities. It supplements its income with local fund-raising.

The Authority is now proposing to build a Community Health Centre, but has also proposed a deal with the Community Council by which the Council will contribute £10,000 – virtually all its existing funds – to this Centre. The Council members want to do this because the money will tip the balance for the Authority building the centre immediately, and should make sure that the building includes a decent nursing surgery, and even a day care room or a play room. It appears that if the Community Council is not willing to put this money in, then the Authority may well defer building indefinitely.

A residents' meeting has been called to discuss the issue, following great pressure on the Community Councillors from those who object to this deal. This meeting has been constituted as an open forum for discussion rather than a formal event. It is not well attended.

There are two possible sites for the proposed centre. One would be adjacent to the existing Community Hall, built on part of the car park and a patch of land that has been turned into an unofficial adventure playground by the local children. The other site could be in the centre of old Eardleigh, next to the pub, where the Authority owns the lease on a garage which operates in what used to be nineteenth-century stables. This building would be demolished.

There is no youth club in Eardleigh, no health clinic, no day centre for the elderly. The Community Hall, a brick and timber building, contains a kitchen and two small meeting rooms, as well as a main hall which seats 120 people. It is underused. There is a body of opinion which believes that more use could be made of it, and that Community funds should be used to encourage this use and to encourage activities.

Some people think that a regular youth club should be set up in the hall, though other residents fear noise and damage. They argue for a separate club building set at the edge of a primary school playing field. However, there are not enough funds to provide this. Yet another group thinks that the Community Hall is not adequate as it is, and should be extended to include recreation rooms, and should be equipped with a proper stage to put on drama and other events. Opinion is also divided as to whether the hall should be permanently licensed for drinking. A few events have been licensed on an individual basis, run by the Community Council, which has always kept a tight grip on what goes on.

Profiles for participants

1. As a committed member of the Labour Party you are firmly against spending any money to pay for facilities that are the responsibility of the Local Authority. You see the Community Council proposal as further evidence of the bad things that happen when one has a Tory-dominated Local Health Authority and Council.

2. As a young mother of two you are all for the Health Centre at any price. Your little boy has speech problems, and it costs you a fortune in bus fares going to the Knighton Clinic. With a new clinic at Eardleigh you could have a speech therapist available at certain times. This is apart from the other general benefits which you also approve of.

3. As a member of the Community Council, and a staunch member of the Conservative Party, you support the plan and the idea of having a Health Centre. You believe that it is right that the community should make some contribution to the Centre. You argue that this would give the residents some say in what facilities go into the Centre and would make them care more about it. You see the deal offered by the Knighton Council as being too good a chance to miss.

4. As a local teacher you are for the Centre and the good that it would do for the community. But you are against putting community money into it – hard-raised and -saved money, as you see it. You feel that if Knighton and the Health Authority can find most of the money for the centre, then they can fund the rest of it if they really want to. You think that the £10,000 from the community is a trivial

amount compared with what you believe it is going to cost (but no one will give exact figures). You would like to see the community cash going into the building of a youth club with recreation facilities, attached to the Community Hall, and built on a self-help basis by local residents.

5. As an older local resident you are against the building of the Centre because of the two sites suggested. You object particularly to the idea of demolishing the 'fine old garage'. You think that the new building would be an eyesore. You cannot see any real need for it anyway. If you want anything, then you get into your car and drive into Knighton, and think that other people should be prepared to do the same. Your doctor provides all the medical support that you need. You would like to see money spent on things like a computer for the primary school or rehanging the church bells, or on reviving the old Eardleigh Fair.

6. As a mother of four, two of them aged two and four years, you would like to see a Health Centre with crèche facilities built next to the Community Hall. You would like to promote and join in with community activities during the day if there was somewhere to leave the children. You believe that there is not enough going on in Eardleigh, which should not be so dependent on Knighton.

7. As the owner of the Corner Stores you quite like the idea of the Health Centre and what it could do for the community, but you wonder if people have thought about things like parking problems, as parking space has not been allowed for in the plans that a friend of yours in the Architects' Department has let you see. He has also told you that the site favoured by the Health Authority is the garage one in the High Street. In any case, you are not keen on spending money on items like the crèche, wherever the centre is placed. You think it should be spent on practical things, like medical equipment.

9 Advertising campaign – group assignment

Situation

You work for an advertising agency. A continental chocolate manufacturer, Lindt, is launching a new chocolate bar similar to Cadbury's *Boost*. It will be priced at about 30 pence retail. Lindt have asked several agencies to prepare a bid for the new account. Your agency has set up a Task Group to prepare an outline campaign and to make a presentation to the client.

Teaching materials

Tasks

The materials you have to produce are:

1 Outline of how you propose to present the product. Decide on a name and a campaign theme.
2 Analysis of the market and your conclusions.
3 Identification of target consumers.
4 Chosen media: the client has indicated that they expect to spend a budget which will include outdoor, magazine and TV media and could include radio. Suggest specified outlets.
5 Prepare 'mock up' advertisements:
   a) magazine page
   b) script/storyboard for TV
   c) specimen tape for radio (one minute or thirty seconds)
   d) poster

In each task you need to explain and justify your proposals. You need to produce a package for the client.

6 Prepare a team presentation for the client to last approximately fifteen minutes. You can use presentation aids like handouts, OHP or flip charts.

Resources

Books; media – magazines etc.; marketing manuals; tape recorders; cameras, if necessary; chocolate bar; yourselves.

Deadline [to be provided]

Figure 4.2 Making display advertisements: procedures of an advertising agency

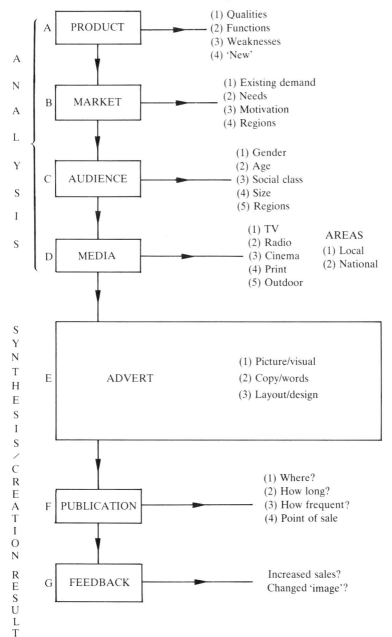

10 Advertising images

The *semantic differential* is a device used by market researchers in order that they can get some idea of the public image of their product.

This is a list of opposing adjectives with a five-point scale in between:

GOOD		X		O		BAD
SOPHISTICATED	O			X		UNSOPHISTICATED
EXCITING	O				X	DULL
HAPPY		O		X		SAD
WEAK				X	O	STRONG
COLD	X				O	HOT
FRIENDLY			X	O		UNFRIENDLY
AGGRESSIVE	O				X	NON-AGGRESSIVE
ACTIVE	O				X	PASSIVE

A group of motor vehicle students were asked to rate two products of the same type on the scale according to where they felt they belonged. The Montego Saloon and the MG Metro Turbo cars were selected as the product. The Montego was marked with an 'X' and the MG Metro with an 'O'. When the task was completed the 'X's and the 'O's were joined up to give a profile of each product.

The students were then challenged to explain how it was that they could so easily describe a conglomeration of bits of metal, glass, plastic, etc. as being 'hot' or 'cold', 'friendly' or 'unfriendly'. From this the idea of a manufactured product image emerged.

11 Newspapers – a comparative study

Your group will be given copies of today's newspapers. From the newspaper you have been given, answer the following questions:

1. Work out the proportions of editorial and advertising content in the newspaper.
2. Calculate the proportions of:
   a. home news
   b. foreign news
   c. sports news
   d. personal interest articles
   e. feature articles (on what topics?)
   f. TV, radio, films and books (previews and reviews)
   g. 'women's articles'

h. leader articles (on what topics?)

i. others.

It may help to count these sections in terms of columns.

3. List the products advertised in the display ads and the probable target population for each advert. List the types of adverts in the classified section.

4. Turn to the lead story:

a. what is the headline?

b. give a brief summary (about twenty to thirty words) of the article and indicate any detectable bias and show what aspects of the story are stressed.

5. Repeat Question 4 with the 'second story'.

6. Choose any page with news articles and list all the adjectives, adverbs and verbs (and nouns if you like) that seem to contain a judgement of a person, group or activity.

7. Choose four photos: list them and their captions. Does each photo illustrate the story, or what other function do they have?

8. Choose a leader, feature or background article: summarize it in forty to fifty words and decide what the purpose of the article is.

9. Sports news: what sports are covered and what information about sports are you given?

10. Write your own definition of 'important news' and of 'trivial news'. Using these definitions, conclude how trivial the newspaper is that you have been analysing. Try to decide what sort of readership it is aimed at.

12 Main points of reference for designing in print media

The following points refer to work in formats such as leaflets, posters, brochures and booklets. These points are in effect a list of items which the student and teacher could look out for when checking the basics of content and treatment. They also serve as a set of criteria headings for assessing such work – to see whether or not they have been taken into account.

Type

Consider size of lettering, especially in relative terms. Consider the typeface and its effect – for example the choice of period lettering with serifs as opposed to modern Helvetica, or even computer print face. Type can also be treated in terms of making choices about use of elements such as bold face or italic or colour.

Teaching materials

Paper

What about the dimensions of the whole piece? Also consider colour, especially if the design demands overprinting in other colours. Perhaps consider the thickness and finish desired for the final product, even details such as deckle edges.

Graphics/illustrations

In this case one is talking mainly about drawings, photographs, charts, but there are also options such as boxes, symbols, list markers, column lines. The former are items which stand as pieces of communication within the whole; the latter contribute to the final look of the product, and help mark out its structure.

Text/copy

Sections of writing can be considered in terms of headings, sub-headings and captions, which mark them out and break them up. There are of course those criteria relating to use of English, such as accuracy and style, but these should also refer back to the idea of appropriateness with reference to audience and purpose in particular.

Layout

The placing of textual and graphic elements on the sheet or page is crucial. Fundamentally, one wishes to achieve clarity, probably by allowing sufficient background space around these elements. To this extent it is essential to learn to draw up layout sheets (see below).

Structure

This applies especially to formats such as the booklet. It is all about the organization, composition and sequence of material. Even on an information poster, for example, which may be relatively heavy on print as opposed to graphics, one can easily talk about structure as the ordering of items down the sheet, the sense of making priorities from top to bottom.

Content

Simply the selection of written and graphic material appropriate to stated purpose and audience needs.

Conventions

One has to take into account general 'rules' for the content and presentation of a given format. For example, it is a convention that a booklet should include elements such as an introduction or numbered pages.

Context

In general this term refers to the physical and social surroundings in which the communication takes place, but in the case of these formats one has to consider two additional glosses on the term. First there is the possibility of context within a larger format. For example, one could design an advertisement to appear within a magazine, in which case it matters as to where it is intended that this advertisement will appear, what will appear before and after it. Second, there is the notion of context as the point of contact with the reader/ viewer. It matters as to whether the communication is to be viewed in the street or at point of sale in a store, for instance. Again, this is likely to affect the treatment of the format. For example, on a basic level, a poster for a notice board has to be big enough to be noticed.

Presentation of these formats

In general, it is worth remembering that one has a choice between preparing a mockup or a layout version of the final product. The mockup is an attempt to produce a version of the communication which looks as close to the ideal result as possible. However, because things like typesetting are beyond most educational resources, it is very difficult to do this perfectly (though the advent of the word processor has made a good deal of difference).

A layout version has three elements: the layout sheets for each page, which show the placing of the text and graphic elements in outline only, e.g. boxes for where they will appear; the text in numbered sections, the numbers being keyed into the boxes on the layout sheets; the illustrations listed and described, or possibly presented as copies. These are also keyed into the space designated on the layout sheet by a code.

Although the layout approach gets round problems of lack of technology and skill, many people still like to produce an attempt at a mockup. But in this case it is still necessary to write additional notes on the final graphic treatment of the materials.

13 A group exercise in genre study

For the purpose of this exercise, you should assume that you are members of a production team working on a popular TV soap opera of your choice. It doesn't matter if you don't know too much about what their jobs involve, but examples of roles could be as follows – producer, director, script editor, script writers, production assistant.

The point of this exercise is to discuss a problem – that your soap is going down in the ratings compared with others. You want to recover your audience, and hold on to your existing audience. You would also like to gain a larger audience.

There has already been general agreement that something needs to be done to heighten the drama, to inject new blood into the characters, while still keeping within the existing formula that has proved popular. Obviously you cannot introduce material that might be considered to be in bad taste or censorable. Nor do you want the changes to go so far that the programme becomes a parody of itself.

Put together some ideas about what you would do, including an outline of a new episode, which you can present to the rest of the class. When you have all exchanged ideas, you could usefully talk over what you have learned about the ideas of formula and of convention in genre.

14 The meaning of birthday cards

Take a look at the reproductions of birthday cards on pp. 120–1. These cards say a lot about gender role and what is valued in our culture. The questions that follow try to get you to see this. Pay attention to any comments on the use of colour in the questions that follow. These cards have lost some of their meaning because they have to be reproduced in black and white.

1. Look at the front of the pair of cards addressed to a son and a daughter. There is a predominance of pastel colours in the card with the little girl. What do you think these cards will suggest to a young girl and young boy about being a girl or a boy? Pay attention to items such as point of view, background, objects with the figures, and what the figures are doing.

2. Look at the pair of cards for six-year-olds. Do any of the points that you made in answer to question 1 still apply? In what way do the written messages also support the contrast between boy and girl birthday cards?

3. Now look at the last pair of cards for young teenagers. There is a predominance of pastels and shading in the female card. It does not actually say that one is for females and one for males – but how do you know that there is this separation? How do the images and the texts reinforce the points that you have already made? In what sense can you see a development through the set of cards, suggesting that boys and girls are being fitted for adult roles? If you have not already said something about this, what value messages do you think are being projected by this third pair of cards?

Here are some simple activities which may teach you something more about your own cultural learning – about the ways in which covert messages and values appear.

4. Design a birthday card for grandmothers – it must be one that you think would really have a chance of selling. Then discuss the meanings and messages that you have created in the light of your answers to the questions above.

5. Now try designing separate cards for mothers and fathers, including the text – but again they must be designs that would really have a chance of selling. When you have done this, try swapping around from one to the other the texts or some part of the images. Does this make a point about gender roles, or stereotyping, or culture and meaning, or conventions?

If this interests you, you might want to take on further activities which involve other 'less obvious' examples of communication, such as the packaging for toys or the packaging of adult goods, or point-of-sale display materials in stores. See if some of the same points are made through these.

15 Use of the library for communication studies (Dewey Classification)

Note that this is a fairly comprehensive list of relevant numbers; there may be only one or two suitable books at any one number. Additional information may be found in encylopaedias.

001	General communication
020	Libraries
029.6	Report writing
070/072	Press and journalism
301.11	Bodily communication

Birthday Wishes,
For a dear SON

Happy Birthday to a Sweet DAUGHTER

Above left and right. Birthday
cards for son and daughter

Right and opposite. Birthday cards
for teenagers

Above left and right. Birthday
cards for six year olds

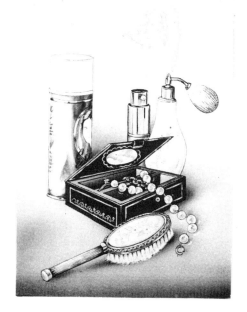

121

301.15	Social communication/Social psychology
301.154	Mass communication
301.44	Subcultures
322.43	Pressure groups
362.4	Handicaps (e.g. deafness, mental handicap)
371.3	Techniques of study
383	Postal services
385	Transport
400	Linguistics (Study of language)
411	Alphabet
420	Language use/English
510.81	Computing (also 615.264)
519	Statistics (for statistical tables see 314.2)
591.5	Animal communication
609	History of technology
651.264	Office machines
651.7	Communication, office services
655.1	History of printing
655.3	Printing processes
655.5	Publishing
658.3	Personnel management
658.45	Communication, management use
658.456	Committee and meetings
658.8	Selling
659	Advertising
659.111	Public relations
659.132	Art in graphics
659.134	Posters
686	Printing and book production
741.64	Book illustration
770	Photography
778.5	Films, production techniques
791.4	Films, entertainment
791.44/45	Broadcasting (radio and TV)
808	Literary composition, including speech (rhetoric)

The library also has:

1 Examples of annual reports of commercial and public bodies
2 Examples of information circulars
3 Examples of periodicals abstracts
4 Library information tools such as the *British National Bibliography*, *British Books in Print*, *British Humanities Index*, *Willings Press Guide*
5 Periodicals, magazines and newspapers

Chapter five

Syllabuses in communication and media studies

In this chapter, we are providing brief summaries and extracts to illustrate the range of communication syllabuses that are currently available. This is by no means an exhaustive collection of all the syllabuses that are available for pupils of school age and for students in further education. But in ranging from City and Guilds Communication Skills, through some vocational education requirements such as secretarial qualifications, BTEC schemes and the Youth Training Scheme and through A level syllabuses, we hope that we can indicate something of the range of what is available.

In the early days of communication studies development, that is through the 1970s, Communication Skills tended to become synonymous with basic English for survival. This tradition continues, but in recent years communication syllabuses have also come to include more serious recognition of (i) the place of interpersonal relationships, group dynamics, and psychological elements of communication, as well as (ii) the technological dimensions of computing and information technology and viewdata systems, along with (iii) audiovisual and mass media work.

Whether the syllabus overleaf is at the Communication Skills end of the spectrum or of the more theoretical Communication Studies type, all of them include both analytical approaches to communication texts and the production of communication artefacts using a variety of media.

We believe that it is possible to identify a discipline of communication that spans the breadth of study from personal communication to mass media. Although the word 'meaning' does not often appear in examination syllabuses, we take the view that at the heart of all these syllabuses and the resulting courses is the attempt to understand how people exchange meanings with one another.

One final note of introduction to this chapter needs to stress that a syllabus is *not* the same as a course of study. Syllabuses have been described simply as 'a licence to examine', or a means of providing certification of what a student has achieved. A syllabus is certainly no more than a skeleton on which a student, usually with the help of a tutor, can create a coherent programme which will provide a range of experiences to develop knowledge, understanding and skills.

GCSE Communication (SEG)

Southern Examining Group, Oxford Office, Ewert House, Ewert Place, Summertown, Oxford OX2 7BZ.

Aims

For GCSE Communication, the aims include the candidate's ability to communicate in as wide a range of media as is practicable but also to explore communication theory through its practical applications. An understanding of how people communicate or fail to communicate as well as the appreciation of good communication and the ability to discriminate between effective and ineffective communication are all primary aims of this syllabus.

Candidates are required to be able to *describe* the content and characteristics of communication and various media; to *interpret* and *apply* their knowledge in various contexts using basic elements of communication theory and showing an awareness of him- or herself as a communicator; and to *perform* and *create* their own communication artefacts working to a set brief, choosing appropriate media and structuring the material for the intended audience.

Target group

As with all GCSE syllabuses, students are expected to take this syllabus in their final years of compulsory schooling and it is also available to candidates at any age above 16.

Content

The syllabus is divided into three sections:

Categories of communication

These are listed as intrapersonal, interpersonal, group, and mass communication. Examples are given of these categories which include, for instance, perception of self and others and the importance of non-verbal communication, aids and barriers to communication, and a range of mass media including new technologies, television and radio, advertising, and film and popular music.

Forms of communication

These are listed under five headings: oral communication, non-verbal communication, written communication, graphical communication (which includes posters, photomontages, video and film sequences) and mass media communication.

Uses of communication

This section includes the various purposes of communication and the different levels at which these purposes might exist, for example, to inform, to entertain, to explain, to persuade, to describe, or to stimulate thought.

Assessment

There are two short written examinations, one of which includes short answer responses and the other includes responding to some case study material.

Students have to complete a project and project folder which includes a complete original, creative piece of communication using one or more media, a working log of progress for this and a commentary evaluating the final product and the methods of working.

As part of this project, there is also an oral assessment in which the candidate presents his or her project to an audience in order to introduce the material, comment on its production, answer questions and lead discussion.

To provide further guidance to teachers for this syllabus, the Southern Examining Group publishes a 'Course Work Memorandum' which gives considerable detail about the expectations of the project and the assessment criteria. There is also a teachers' guide which gives a good deal of useful background information about teaching the syllabus and assessing the course work.

GCE A Level Communication Studies (AEB)

Associated Examining Board, Stag Hill House, GUILDFORD, Surrey GU2 5XJ

A Level Communication Studies was first examined in 1978 when there were 100 candidates. Ten years later in 1988 there were 3,000 candidates. At the time of writing this is the only established communication studies or media studies syllabus at A level and is now accepted by most British universities and all polytechnics and colleges of higher education. Other A-level examining boards are currently preparing media studies syllabuses and information about one of these is available in this chapter.

Aims

There is a substantial list of objectives for this A level but the overall aim is summed up quite briefly: 'to promote *knowledge* of, *understanding* of and *competence* in communication by study of categories, forms and uses of communication in order to interpret major theories and issues; *application* of this study to cases drawn from authentic situations; and *development of practical skills* in communication'. This A level is firmly placed as a combination of (i) analytical and (ii) practical, creative work, (iii) a theoretical study of communication theories and issues and (iv) the development of communication skills through case study approaches and a practical project to produce a piece of communication.

Target group

This is the same as for all A level subjects. It is intended normally to be followed as a post-GCSE two-year course for eighteen-year-olds or for mature students.

Content

The syllabus is divided into five major sections, each of which is described in some detail with examples. These sections are:

Categories of communication

Includes: intrapersonal; interpersonal; extrapersonal (communication through and to non-human and inanimate sources); group communication; and mass communication.

Forms of communication

Organized under the subheadings of oral, written and printed, non-verbal (which includes effects and uses of body language, dress and display cues), graphical (which includes pictorial and symbolic modes), numerical (which includes the presentation and interpretation of numerical data) and new technologies (which includes applications of information technology).

Use of communication

Includes information gathering, storage and retrieval; persuasion, propaganda and publicity; entertainment; socialization; and social functioning. Socialization includes the ways in which communication plays a part in constructing social reality and in the acquisition of individual roles; social functioning includes issues of expressive needs and personal growth and creative expression in the arts.

Theory in communication studies

Includes the identification of basic factors, description of principles, and the uses and limitations of models. Students are expected to be able to describe and interpret communication processes and the development of mass communications since the late nineteenth century, and current developments into the future.

Issues in communication studies

Includes matters of public debate within political, economic, social and cultural spheres.

Hence the syllabus for this A level is a wide-ranging one, covering issues of personal communications as well as mass media studies.

Assessment

The assessment of this A level is in three parts. There are two externally set examinations. Paper 1 consists of questions which require an essay-type response, although some may specify short answer or note form questions and invite graphical as well as literary responses. This examination carries 40 per cent of the total marks. Paper 2 consists of one or two case studies for which materials are given to candidates in advance of the examination. Candidates are then asked to use those materials as the basis of analytical work such as the creation of storyboards, reports, letters, questionnaires, and so on. This paper carries 30 per cent of the total marks. The third aspect of the assessment is a practical project for which a candidate or group of candidates is required to create a communication artefact in a chosen medium or media such as slide-tape, print, video, radio, etc. There is also an oral presentation to a group in order to relate the project work and its production to a group of people. The project and associated oral carry 30 per cent of the marks.

There are further notes of guidance available for teachers about the syllabus and project work. There are also resource lists available and a network of regional working parties which organize conferences and support groups for teaching communication studies.

GCSE Media Studies (SEG)

University of Oxford Delegacy of Local Examinations, Ewert Place, Summertown, OXFORD OX2 7BZ

Aims

The aims include the fostering of a critical appreciation of what people say and hear in the media; a critical awareness of media representations of individuals, groups and issues; comprehension of the development and functioning of the media organizations and the consequent influence of their products; an awareness of the debate about the effects of the media; and enabling the candidates to construct their own representations of their ideas and experiences using one or more media.

Target group

The target group is the same as all GCSE syllabuses.

Content

The content for this syllabus is expressed very broadly. The media are defined as television, radio, films, newspapers and magazines; but can also include what are described as 'fringe' media such as popular music, cartoons, comics, etc.

In addition to this definition of the media, a list of themes is suggested which, in turn, is described as not being exhaustive and teachers may wish to add other themes. The themes which are listed in the syllabus are: image analysis, advertising, stereotyping/representation, making of personalities, genre/style, minority groups, news production/values, balance and bias, constraints/controls/ownership/access/revenue, audience, regional/international comparisons and influences, and new technology.

Candidates are also expected to become familiar with the principal technical processes involved in media production such as camera angles, picture composition, video editing, sound editing, storyboard and scripting and so on.

Assessment

Assessment is through course work assignments and practical project. Examples of potential course work assignments are given, for example, comparison of two magazine advertisements for perfume, each appealing to a different market. The practical project consists of a media production and an accompanying production log.

The details of subject content, course work assignments and practical project are all left fairly open in the syllabus for teachers and candidates to develop themselves.

Within the course work there must be six assignments of equal weighting, testing all of the specified assessment objectives. These assignments are internally assessed and externally moderated by the Southern Examining Group. The same is true of the practical project. Course work accounts for 150 marks and the project accounts for 75 marks. A course work memorandum for teachers provides guidance on the centre-assessed components.

GCSE Media Studies (NEA)

Joint Matriculation Board, MANCHESTER M15 6EU

Aims

The aims of this syllabus range widely and include developing the four main language skills of talking, listening, reading and writing; participating in creative and analytical work; developing group and social skills through working as members of a team solving the problems of production; developing a spirit of enquiry, aesthetic awareness, a faculty for self-assessment, and an understanding of the significance of the media for different groups in society; developing knowledge of the financial institutional organizations which constitute the media; and putting skill and understanding of media processes into practice with the production of appropriate media texts. The term 'media texts' refers to any written or audio/visual media.

Target group

The target group is as for all GCSE syllabuses.

Content

Six study areas are listed for detailed analysis: media languages; media audiences; genre; ownership, control and prevailing ideologies; production; representation. These six study areas are intended to provide the analytical framework for studying any two or more of the listed media, which are films, television, radio, newspapers, popular music, magazines and comics.

A more detailed list of topics within each of the six study areas is provided; and most usefully of all each of these six study areas is tabulated under each of the media to indicate topics and possible teaching strategies for dealing with the subject content. These tables of content do, in fact, provide a very useful summary of key areas of content for media studies, not only for GCSE, but at any level.

Assessment

The assessment takes the form of six pieces of course work and one practical project – that is a minimum requirement. The six items of course work consist of five items which meet the requirements of the specific objectives and must include work on at least two different media such as the production processes used in the chosen media. The practical project consists of a piece of practical work accompanied by an account of the production process. This practical work can be produced either by an individual or by a group. The final marks are awarded as 60 per cent for the folder of course work and 40 per cent for the practical project work.

The Northern Examining Association also publishes background information for teachers under the heading 'approaching project work'. This leaflet suggests examples of particular types of practical projects within the media of the print, video, and film. There is also detail of the assessment criteria including ways of assessing group project work.

The Northern Examining Association offers two GCSE media studies syllabuses. Both are virtually identical in terms of content and assessment, but Syllabus B is organized in modules which specify the topic areas for the course work assignments. These are: module 1 media language, module 2 mediation/representation, module 3 institutions, module 4 audience, module 5 a unifying double project. This final double project takes the form of a practical project undertaken individually or as a member of a group.

The GCSE syllabuses which have been summarized here, i.e., the Southern Examining Group and Northern Examining Association, are only two of those available. Other GCSE examining groups also offer GCSE Media Studies.

GCE A Level Media Studies (University of Cambridge)

University of Cambridge Local Examinations Syndicate, Syndicate Buildings, 1 Hills Road, CAMBRIDGE CB1 2EU

The University of Cambridge Local Examinations Syndicate is currently developing A Level Media Studies within two syllabuses. Syllabus A will be examined for the first time in the summer of 1990. Syllabus B, which is a modular syllabus, is still under consideration by the Secondary Examinations and Assessment Council. The following notes refer to Media Studies A Level Syllabus A.

Aims

The aims of this syllabus are grouped into three headings:

1   To provide students with an integrated conceptual understanding of media products, the practices which lead to their production, the institutions in which they are produced and the audiences who meet with them.
2   To provide students with an analytical and critical framework for understanding the differences and similarities between media products, practices, institutions and audiences.
3   To encourage students to develop critical approaches to the media in selective historical moments, social frameworks, geographical locations and aesthetic forms.

The overall aims of this syllabus are the analysis of media products and a critical understanding of the processes and practices involved in the media.

Target group

This is the same as for all A-level subjects.

Content

The content of this syllabus is divided into three main sections:

Reading skills/textual analysis

Within this area five aspects are stressed. These are image analysis, which includes both still images and moving images; genre analysis, which includes the concept of genre and comparative case studies from fictional and non-fictional genres; narrative analysis, which includes literary and visual fictional analysis; representation which includes case studies in media representation of two categories from gender, race, class, age or sexuality; production exercises which will include images in context such as a portfolio of photographs or a storyboard, a non-fiction product, such as a magazine or radio or video news, and exercises in style, for example melodrama or expressions, or a free choice production which the candidate can choose.

Institutions

This section of the syllabus is again divided into five parts: media sociology; international organization of the press and image markets; concepts of alternative and independent institutions, for example, the alternative press, or the Jamaican music industry; the concept of audience; and two selective case studies for four options which will be specified annually. Examples of these case studies are production and presentation of news in Britain, or the USA studio system of film making.

Media debates

Examples of these debates include television drama, European avant-garde practices, teenage magazines, or the British documentary movement. Additionally, studies of debate around issues such as ideology or popular culture and from the manufacture of news or cultural nationalism.

In line with other syllabuses in communication or media studies, notes for this syllabus indicate the technology that should be available for teaching. The statement indicates the following: 'The syllabus therefore caters for centres with high tech facilities (e.g. television studio systems and/or desk top publishing); low tech facilities (e.g. portapack video cameras and/or slide/tape technology) and even lower tech facilities (e.g. only software provision for storyboarding and/or newspaper simulations)'.

Assessment

The assessment is based on three papers set and marked by the University of Cambridge Local Examinations Syndicate. Paper 1 will be a three-hour paper to answer four questions in two sections: section A media institutions, and section B media debates. This will carry 30 per cent of the marks.

Paper 2 is completed in the students' own time and consists of a package of four exercises or artefacts from the sections of the syllabus. The package will be accompanied by a commentary of approximately 2,000 words, critically accounting for the processes through which the contents of the package were selected and produced. This will be submitted at the same time as Paper 1 and will carry 40 per cent of the marks.

Paper 3, again completed in the students' own time, will be an analysis of one prescribed contemporary film, television programme, newspaper issue, etc., in its institutional context. This analysis will be approximately 3,000 words long and the requirements will be specified by the examination board at the start of the September term in the year of examination. This essay must be submitted by 1 May of the year of the examination.

Hence, 60 per cent of the assessment is broadly based on analysis of media products, institutions and debates, and 40 per cent is based on the production of materials.

Communication Skills (City and Guilds)

City and Guilds of London Institute, 76 Portland Place, LONDON W1N 4AA

The City and Guilds of London Institute introduced Communication Skills syllabuses in the late 1970s. These were, in the early days, used in Colleges of Further Education, but in recent years have also been used at secondary school level.

There was some controversy about these syllabuses, since they seemed to be replacing the broad-based general studies or liberal studies tradition with a rather more narrow focus on functional skills of communication. However, most teachers and lecturers would now accept that these syllabuses provide a framework of assessment through course work and set assignments which can be used as a vehicle for introducing a broad range of personal, social, cultural and work-based contexts and issues.

There are now Communication Skills certificates at three levels. Each of these levels includes four elements: reading, listening, writing and speaking. The broad aims of these certificates are the same, but the individual syllabuses indicate a wider range of contexts, of skills and of judgement as one moves up to Level 3.

Aims

The overall aim of these Communication Skills syllabuses is to certificate students' proficiency in a range of communication skills, and their ability to judge when and how to apply these skills in a range of vocational, educational and social contexts relevant to their individual needs. The phrase that occurs throughout the aims of these syllabuses is 'communicative competence'. For example, the aims at Level 3 include 'communicative competence in familiar and unfamiliar and public situations involving a wide range of people; in initiating and sustaining effective communication with the individuals and groups of various types; in tackling open-ended communication problems requiring a critical appraisal of the options available within the situation'.

Target group

Candidates for this certification are usually at the 16+ and adult level, but they can be taken prior to the school leaving age. It is made clear that there are no specific educational pre-requirements for people to take these certificates.

Content

As indicated above, there are four sections to each of the Communication Skills certificates at Levels 1, 2 and 3.

Receive and interpret information in written and graphical forms

The focus of this is the reading and understanding of a variety of texts, including tabular and graphical presentation, and including the ability to identify emotive words and phrases and to distinguish between fact and opinion. At Level 3, issues such as the recognition of implicit meanings, different attitudes and roles in a writer and the evaluation of the effectiveness of the material with respect to intended audience and purposes are included.

Receive and interpret information in oral form

The range of skills identified here includes the ability to listen in a responsive manner and to identify non-verbal factors including tone, style and body language. Once again, at Level 3, the evaluation of material and the identification of assumed values are included.

Communicate effectively in written graphical form

This section includes skills such as describing, making notes, writing letters, completing forms, using graphical forms such as sketch maps and diagrams. At Level 3, the syllabus includes the selection and use of the most effective and appropriate combination of written, graphical and tabular forms to put forward a logical/effective argument in support of a factual statement, point of view or opinion.

Communicate effectively in oral form

This section includes speaking audibly and distinctly in order to explain and describe situations and to express opinion. The use of tabular and graphical data is also included. Once again, at Level 3, the ability to evaluate effectiveness is included.

The City and Guilds syllabuses present a useful analysis of a range of basic communication skills. They do not specifically include analysis of media materials or of visual materials in the sense of art and photography. However, the background information for the certificates includes useful references to the resources required, the media and the contexts that should be used. With regard to equipment, the syllabus is quite clear: 'ideally a well-equipped base room should be available, containing, for example, practice telephones, video and audio recorders, course work materials in written and graphic form, writing and drawing equipment, and facilities for basic computing or typing. The minimum requirement will be access to tape or video recorders, the provision of writing and drawing equipment, and the storage of assignment materials'.

Assessment

At all three levels the assessment is by course work which is devised by the centre, and compulsory assignments which are devised by the City and Guilds of London Institute.

Specific examples of such course work are indicated. For example, at Level 3, such course work should show evidence of personal autonomy through tackling open-ended communication problems and should include work that is designed, planned and executed by groups of students.

The criteria for assessment are usefully laid out as 'The effectiveness of the communication in relation to its intended audience and purpose'. Additionally, at Level 3, as well as communicating effectively at a functional level, candidates also need to be able to evaluate the processes and products which are being produced. However, the syllabus does not specifically talk about the need for identifying principles, theories or models of communication in order to do this. All of the tasks are at a primary functional level rather than a reflective or theoretical level.

Multi-task assignments are required as part of the course work, and within the syllabus area of receiving and interpreting information in written and graphical forms, a large list of examples for media and contexts of work is given. These include written and graphic symbolic and numerical material including books, advertisements, instruction manuals, notices, newspapers, technical journals, memos and so on, including viewdata systems.

Communication in BTEC

The Business and Technician Education Council (BTEC), Central House, Upper Woburn Place, LONDON WC1H 0HH.

The Business and Technician Education Council (BTEC) was formed in 1983 from the merger of the Business Education Council (BEC) and the Technician Education Council (TEC). In the late 1970s and early 1980s BEC and TEC were responsible for a good deal of development in the teaching and learning of communication work in post-16 vocational education. The module known as 'People and Communication' which was developed by BEC aimed to develop students' communication knowledge and skills and their application in business environments. This scheme moved beyond the 'use of English in business' to include areas such as non-verbal communication issues within business organizations. TEC did not publish a required syllabus for 'General and Communication Studies' in TEC programmes, but laid down general criteria which centres had to follow in order to ensure that 15 per cent of a technician education course was dealing with communication, both personal and employment-based, and more general social, cultural and economic issues.

The booklet published by BTEC in September 1984 with the title *Policies and Priorities into the 1990s* marked a new era in vocational education. BTEC is currently responsible for validating vocational education for a very wide range of career areas. There are nine boards within BTEC as follows: agricultural subjects; business and finance; computing and information systems; construction; design; distributive, hotel and catering and leisure services; engineering; public administration; and science.

BTEC qualifications are available at four main levels. These are the Certificate in Pre-Vocational Education (which is jointly certificated with the City and Guilds); First Level, National Level, and Higher National Level. There are also units of Continuing Education available for adults who have previous business experience.

The certificates and diplomas for BTEC are now very largely integrated into a coherent programme of learning and development and do not consist of separate subject areas. Common skills and core themes are woven through these integrated programmes.

It is not possible to generalize about all BTEC courses from each of the nine boards. In this section we shall merely refer to some of the current documents for some of the career areas, and indicate how communication knowledge and skills are part of the common skills element and core themes which are required by BTEC.

A general guideline on these common skills and core themes was published in July 1986, and provides a useful list of the major common skill areas which students are expected to develop: self-development skills; communicating and working with others (which includes presenting information effectively for a particular purpose; listening to and interpreting information/communications; relating to others, negotiating, making/accepting criticism; working in a team and taking a variety of roles); problem-tackling, decision-making and investigating; information, quantitative and numerical skills (which includes obtaining a range of information for a specific purpose and using a range of techniques to analyse data and present complex information); and practical skills.

It is clear, therefore, that these common skills include a good deal of communication-oriented work. This is highlighted through a specimen skills statement in which the section headed 'Communication' has this note: 'Communication skills should be given high priority in skills development programmes'. This section then goes on to list what are described as areas that tend to be under-emphasized and these include: the preparation and execution of a wide variety of types of communication such as oral/written/formal/ informal; the identification of purpose, contexts and the intended recipients of a message employing appropriate form, structure, language, style and tone; the ability to use and interpret non-verbal elements, for example, gestures, expressions, body language, and to use illustrative material such as visual, graphic, numerical or aural; the ability to identify likely causes of breakdown in communication and to assess the effectiveness of one's own and other people's communication.

These themes of communication, such as the forms of written, spoken and non-verbal communication, the assessment of different media, and the recognition of judging the effectiveness of communication, are all stressed throughout BTEC programmes. The other crucial aspect, with regard to BTEC and communication elements, is the way in which BTEC programmes are delivered. BTEC itself has published a good deal of material to illustrate how students are expected to develop the necessary knowledge and skills to be effective as individuals and in teams in their places of work. The prime learning method is through assignments which integrate the various knowledge areas in order to apply knowledge to specific business situations. The example of a course outline for a BTEC National programme in Chapter 2 gives some indication of this assignment-based approach. Communication work is not a separate element, but rather a common area throughout the course whatever occupational area is involved.

All BTEC courses are internally assessed by the teachers on the course and externally assessed by visiting moderators.

To indicate the range of content which is expected under the heading of 'Communication' on a BTEC programme, the core unit 'People in Organizations' has the following main sections:

Understand the principal features of organizational structures and operations and how these affect the communications system of an organization

Give and exchange information
This section includes a long list of communication for business

purposes: oral and written information, personal exchanges, telephone techniques; types and formats of main business documents; understanding information systems and information flows; information and control of organizations; the organization's internal communication methods, e.g. memoranda, notices, personal exchanges; the organization's external methods of communication, e.g. letter, telephone, telex; interpretation of statistical and financial and graphical information, e.g. stock movements, absenteeism, interest rates; identification from information of trends and likely outcomes; development of materials relating to advertisements, job preparation or applications, e.g. job descriptions, curricula vitae, etc.

Examine information systems and their impact on an organization's operations, in terms of the use of a range of formats for information handling

Assess the uses of electronic technology as a means of communication

Present and disseminate information, using appropriate means

Appreciate the importance of personal relationships and a social environment

This section includes: verbal and non-verbal communication; social skills in the work context, e.g. recognizing and adopting appropriate behaviour in specific business situations; flexible response to personal factors; interviewing and counselling skills; adaptation of messages to the needs of different recipients; factors that influence the process and effectiveness of groups; effective presentation of ideas, e.g. persuasion, selling ideas, group discussion, customer/client contact.

Recognize factors which contribute to efficient work within an organization and ways in which this can be assessed and influenced

Assess the relationship between the working environment and the employee's performance

Identify the constraints and opportunities of group working, sources of conflict and methods of conflict management

Analyse changes which affect the work of individuals and groups within organizations

Communication in YTS

Like BTEC, the Youth Training Scheme is a very broad-based national scheme. It is funded by the Training Agency and is not specifically a communications syllabus. However, we believe that it is worthwhile spending a moment looking at the results which are expected for trainees on this scheme, which includes a good deal of attention to what we consider to be the skills elements within communication.

The four aims for the Youth Training Scheme are:

Competence in a job and/or range of occupational skills

This element involves specific job skills and competencies but also a broader knowledge and understanding of the world of work, its rules and customs, and roles within it.

Competence in a range of transferable core skills

The core areas in YTS are defined as number and its application, communication, problem-solving and planning, practical skills, and computer and information technology.

Ability to transfer skills and knowledge to new situations

In order to transfer skills and knowledge, the trainee needs to develop a grasp of the underlying principles of tasks and be exposed to unfamiliar situations so that he or she can practise and demonstrate the redeployment of skills and knowledge already acquired.

Interpersonal effectiveness

This is described as involving the development of initiative, the ability to handle interpersonal relationships, the acceptance of responsibility and the development of self-sufficiency. It is also worth noting that the Youth Training Scheme documentation stresses that to make a full use of interpersonal effectiveness, trainees will need an appreciation about the world outside work.

In briefly indicating these four areas of development for trainees within the YTS, we would want to stress the core skill of communication, the highlighting of interpersonal relationships, and the use of work-based and other contexts.

Communication in secretarial examinations (LCCI)

London Chamber of Commerce and Industry Examinations Board,

Marlowe House, Station Road, SIDCUP, Kent DA15 7BJ

The LCCI provides certification for secretarial qualifications at various levels. For each of these group secretarial certificates (such as the Private and Executive Secretaries Diploma or the Secretarial Studies Certificate) there is an element within the course entitled 'Communication'. This communication element is integrated into the study required for the secretarial certificates, and can be combined with shorthand transcription or audio transcription within the context of the business organization.

In the context of these diplomas, communication encompasses use of English, meetings, and transcription, either from audio or from shorthand. The purpose of the use of English, which is examined through an externally-set written paper, is 'To ensure that the candidate is able to demonstrate the high degree of competence in the handling of English expected at a secretarial level'.

For the Private and Executive Secretary Diploma, the examination paper in the use of English tests the ability to compose letters, reports or other business documents from data provided. It also includes the ability to summarize facts, opinions, arguments and counter-arguments in any given passage. It also includes the interpretation and action required which may include the necessity to infer a line of argument or to discern an intention of the writer which may not be overtly stated.

The meetings section of the communication work is dependent on a video tape of a meeting concerning a company known as Comlon International Plc. From this video tape, the candidate has to record the business conducted and produce, using a keyboard, a report summary or minutes of the meeting, conference, debate or lecture on the video tape which may last from twenty to twenty-five minutes.

Other aspects of this group certificate, such as secretarial administration, also include aspects of communication in organizations. These will include the means by which business communication is relayed within and outside a company. It includes aspects of public relations and the use of media for companies, for example, the characteristics and comparative costing of various media.

In addition to secretarial certificates and diplomas, the LCCI also offers individual subject examinations, one of which is entitled 'English for Business'. This examination is available at three different levels. The third and most advanced level aims to test a high-level ability to understand, write and use the general and special varieties of English used in business and the ability to use the appropriate formats. The three-hour examination tests the candidate's ability to compose a letter from incoming data; to draft an internal report based on raw data; a comprehension task based on a piece of communication such as a press article or a company report; and the conversion of the message from one format to another, for example, the production of a memo from a telex cable or a computer printout.

Communication in Business (RSA)

Royal Society of Arts Examinations Board, Murray Road, ORPINGTON, Kent, BR5 3RB

The RSA Certificates for Communication in Business are available at three levels: stage 1 elementary, stage 2 intermediate and stage 3 advanced. These reflect the usual stages for RSA examinations in which stage 2 is normally considered to be approximately equal to the higher grades of GCSE. Stages 1 and 2 are similar syllabuses with the same name sections, however, at stage 2 there are additional and more complex expectations. Stage 3 assumes that the topics of stage 2 are all included and then goes into new topic areas. Thus we shall look at stages 1 and 2 together and then at stage 3 separately.

Aims for stages 1 and 2

The intention of this certificate is to demonstrate students' competence in undertaking a number of communicating functions which business organizations require of individuals.

Target group

At stage 1 there are no specific requirements except a basic competence in written and spoken English adequate for the demands of the course. At stage 2 the same competence is assumed at a level equivalent to stage 1.

Content

Both stage 1 and stage 2 syllabuses are divided into four parts: (i) principles and processes of communication which include communication systems in business, relationships in business, and a basic understanding of new technology; (ii) oral and non-verbal communication which includes the use of the telephone and the ability to present a prepared topic to a group; (iii) written communication which includes letters, memoranda, summaries, advertisements and business forms; (iv) use of English which includes textual accuracy, punctuation, grammar, vocabulary, spelling and style.

Assessment

There is a written examination which carries 80 per cent of the marks and an oral test which carries 20 per cent of the marks.

Aims for stage 3

The aims of this examination are to test understanding of communication at an advanced level in business organizations and the application of the underlying principles of communication in practical business situations.

Target group

This is intended for full-time and part-time students in schools and colleges and could be used for students who are updating their skills. Students will have achieved RSA stage 2 or equivalent or have experience.

Contents

This syllabus includes all the stage 2 topic areas and in addition five new sections: (i) receiving and storing communications, which includes processes of perception, listening skills and technological storage systems; (ii) sending communications, which includes oral and writing skills; (iii) decision-making, which includes the processes of collecting information, analysing, implementing and evaluating; (iv) principles and processes of communication, which include elementary models, communication chains, appreciation of information technology and the mass media; (v) human relations, which includes personal issues such as motivation and prejudices and group dynamics within organizations.

Assessment

There are three parts to the assessment. First, there is a case-study type project leading to a report. Second, there is a viva based on the project. These two elements carry 50 per cent of the marks. Third, there is a written paper which tests ability to handle information in a practical way and also general understanding of communication issues in business.

RSA Communication in Business at stage 3 is a wide-ranging syllabus which leads into theoretical perspectives of interpersonal, group, organizational and mass communication as well as to development of practical skills.

Chapter six

Resources and sources of information

This brief resource list is confined to books and other materials and sources of information which are intended for *teaching* communication and media studies; and to materials mentioned in this text. We refer you to bibliographies elsewhere and to the publishers listed below for more general materials. In particular, you will find useful resource lists in books mentioned below by Alvarado, Gutch and Wollen, Burton and Dimbleby, and Masterman. We have also included addresses of agencies which produce materials or organize events and exhibitions.

Books

Alvarado, M., Gutch, R., Wollen, T. (1987) *Learning the Media: An introduction to media teaching* London: Macmillan

Argyle, M. (1983) *The Psychology of Interpersonal Behaviour* 4th edn Harmondsworth: Penguin

——— (1987) *Bodily Communication* 2nd edn London: Methuen

Barker, L. (1986) *Communication* New York: Prentice Hall

Bond, T. (1986) *Games for Social and Life Skills* London: Hutchinson

Brandes, D. (1981) *The Gamesters' Handbook* London: Hutchinson Educational

Brandes, D. and Phillips, H. (1978) *Gamesters' Handbook* London: Hutchinson Educational

Burton, G. and Dimbleby, R. (1988) *Between Ourselves: An introduction to interpersonal communication* London: Edward Arnold

Butterworth, C. and MacDonald, M. (1985) *Teaching Social Education and Communication* London: Hutchinson

Clarke, M. (1987) *Teaching Popular Television* London: Heinemann Educational Books

Collins, G. (1987) *Case Studies in Communication* London: Pitman

Cook, P. (ed.) (1986) *The Cinema Book* London: BFI

Crisell, A. (1986) *Understanding Radio* London: Methuen

Curran, J. and Seaton, J. (1987) *Power Without Responsibility: The Press and Broadcasting in Britain* 3rd edn, London: Methuen

De Vito, J. (1986) *Human Communication* New York: Harper and Row

Dimbleby, R. and Burton, G. (1985) *More Than Words: An introduction to communication* London: Methuen

Dyer, G. (1982) *Advertising as Communication* London: Methuen

Evans, D. (1987) *People, Communication and Organizations* London: Pitman

Fiske, J. (1982) *Introduction to Communication Studies* London: Methuen

———— (1987) *Television Culture* London: Methuen

Goffman, E. (1959) *The Presentation of Self in Everyday Life* Harmondsworth: Penguin

Goodwin, A., Cook, J., and North, N. (eds) (1988) *Media Studies for Adults* London: BFI

Gration, G.N., Titford, J., and Reilly, J. (1988) *A First Course in Communication and Media Studies* London: Macmillan

Hackman, S. and H. (1987) *Television Studies* London: Hodder and Stoughton

Harris, J. and Bell, V. (1987) *People in Organisations* London: Pitman

Hood, S. (1983) *On Television* 2nd edn. London: Pluto Press

Hopson, B. and Scally, M. (1981) *Teaching Social and Life Skills* London: McGraw-Hill

Jones, K. (1985) *Design Your Own Simulations* London: Methuen

Life Skills Teaching Programmes (1981) Life Skills Associates, Ashlings, Back Church Lane, Leeds LS16 8DN. (A series of ring binders with resource materials and activities for social and life skills.)

Lorac, C. and Weiss, M. (1981) *Communication and Social Skills*, Exeter: Wheaton

Lusted, D. and Drummond, P. (1985) *TV and Schooling* London: BFI

Lusted, D. (ed.) (1988) *The Media Studies Book – A Guide for Teachers* London: Comedia and BFI

McKeown, N. (1982) *Case Studies and Projects in Communication* London: Methuen

Masterman, L. (1980) *Teaching about Television* London: Macmillan

———— (1986) *Teaching the Media* 2nd edn, London: Comedia

Montgomery, M. (1986) *An Introduction to Language and Society* London: Methuen

Morgan, J. and Welton, P. (1986) *See What I Mean: An introduction to visual communication* London: Edward Arnold

Myers, G.E. and Myers, M.T. (1986) *The Dynamics of Human Communication*, 4th edn, New York: McGraw-Hill
———— (1982) *Managing by Communication: An organisational approach* New York: McGraw-Hill
Myers, K. (1986) *Understains: The sense and seduction of advertising* London: Methuen
O'Sullivan, T. (1983) *Key Concepts in Communication* London: Methuen
Stanton, N. (1982) *What do you mean 'Communication'? An organisational approach* New York: McGraw-Hill
Watson, J. (1985) *What is Communication Studies?* London: Edward Arnold
Watson, J. and Hill, A. (1989) *Dictionary of Communication and Media Studies* London: Edward Arnold

Other materials

In this section we are including a range of printed materials in non-book form along with various audio-visual resources. They are listed according to publisher.

British Broadcasting Corporation, Broadcasting House, London W1A 1AA

The BBC obviously provides an enormous range of resources for students of communication and media. More specifically, there is the annual report which gives a good deal of factual data about the whole range of BBC services; there is a termly menu of educational broadcasts with supporting documentation – recently this has included regular series such as *Inside Television* (videos of this are available from BBC TV Schools Broadcasting, Villiers House, The Broadway, London W5 2PA), and of course there are the weekly publications *The Listener* and *Radio Times*. It is possible to obtain tapes of some BBC productions from BBC Enterprises Limited, Woodlands, 80 Wood Lane, London W12 0TT. BBC Enterprises has also published a learning package entitled *Get It Taped: The video camera in school* which comprises a video tape, a booklet and an audio tape to introduce students to basic techniques of video production using a minimum amount of equipment.

British Film Institute Education Department, 21 Stephen Street, London W1P 1PL

The annual publications catalogue will give you full details of all of their published materials which are designed for use in schools and colleges. For example, *Reading Pictures* (photos, slides and notes for image analysis); *Selling Pictures* (photos, slides and notes offer an introduction to representation and stereotyping); *The Companies You Keep* (booklet and photos on commercial media institutions and ownership); *Semiology of the Image* (slides and notes for reading images: although the original material is now somewhat dated it still provides an excellent approach to this area of work and can be used to stimulate further study). The BFI is a unique source of film and TV materials such as extracts and study packs including *Teaching Coronation Street*; *Hammer Horror: A cinema case study*; *The Dumb Blonde Stereotype*; *Criminal Records*; *Teaching TV Crime Series*; *TV Title Sequences*, and many more.

Basil Blackwell Publisher, PO Box 87, Oxford OX4 1LB

Blackwell publishes a series of simulations by Ken Jones for developing oral and written communication skills which can include audio and video tape presentation. The documentation provides role play situations in which the participants resolve the problems in which they find themselves.

Cambridge University Press, The Pitt Building, Trumpington Street, Cambridge CB2 1RP

The Communications Kit (1989) by Tom Banks and Jane Weston provides a useful ring file of photocopiable materials to encourage students to make practical explorations into the forms of communication used in our society. All of it is well developed and well tried to present an activity-based introduction to the theoretical background.

Channel 4 Television, 60 Charlotte Street, London W1P 2AX

Many productions for Channel 4 and the associated printed materials are useful for communication work. The *Open the Box: A new way of looking at television* series is noteworthy. The book is published by Routledge/Comedia and the programmes are available from the British Film Institute Film and Video Library, 21 Stephen Street, London W1P 1PL. Additionally programmes broadcast for the Open College on Channel 4 have relevant material for communication work.

Careers and Occupational Information Centre (COIC), Training Agency, Room W1101, Moorfoot, Sheffield S1 4PQ

This arm of the former Manpower Services Commission publishes primarily careers-related literature including information on media careers. But in addition to this, it also publishes some teaching (or rather 'training') materials which can be helpful to the communication teacher. One example of this is a booklet entitled *Working Together! A handbook for adult groups* which is a mine of ideas and activities for developing group work and group identity and for enabling people to build their abilities to work in groups.

Independent Broadcasting Authority, 70 Brompton Road, London SW3 1EY

The IBA publishes an annual report about British commercial radio and television, and also a range of factual leaflets about the independent broadcasting system. At the Brompton Road headquarters there is also a gallery for free group visits with exhibitions about TV and radio production. There is also a free quarterly magazine, *Airwaves*, which contains useful articles on issues of current concern in broadcasting. Educational broadcasting is produced by the ITV companies and the termly menus usually include media-related series, for example the recent *Understanding Television* programmes and accompanying booklets.

The Industrial Society, Peter Runge House, 3 Carlton House Terrace, London SW1Y 5DG

In addition to organizing courses and conferences, The Industrial Society also publishes materials, including a series of booklets entitled *Communication Skills Guides* on *Effective Meetings*, *Effective Speaking*, *Interviewing*, *Letter Writing*, *Rapid Reading*, *Report Writing*, and *Telephone Techniques*. They are clearly and concisely written with practical advice and techniques as well as examples.

Leicestershire Media Education Project, Centre for Educational Technology, Merrick Road, Leicester LE2 6DJ

Amongst the materials produced by this project is a four-part video called *Media Kids OK* which gives an idea of the range of activities which media education can include in the primary school.

Macmillan Education Limited, Houndmills, Basingstoke, Hampshire RG21 2XS

The Media Pack by Stephen Kruger and Ian Wall is a ring binder collection of teaching materials particularly for GCSE Media Studies. There are lots of practical ideas and activities on TV, film, the news, advertising, pop music, radio, language, genre, representation, ownership, finance, production, and audience. Macmillan also publish a collection of communication and life skills assignments which provide useful documents and situations for 'functional' oral and written work.

Mary Glasgow Publications Limited, Brookhampton Lane, Kineton, Warwick, CV35 0BR

Mary Glasgow tends to specialize in materials for foreign language teaching, but several publications are particularly relevant to students of communication and media: *Talking Pictures – An introduction to media studies* is a slide-tape sequence prepared by Peter Barker and Mike Clarke which explains several themes and analytical techniques; *Eyewitness – Whose point of view?* is a slide-tape sequence on documentary; *Mediafile* is available on annual subscription for three termly issues for teachers concerned with media education at 14–16+ level, usually consisting of six to eight pages of units of pupil's resource material and teacher's notes and one practical or topical unit; and *The Media Manual* which is a practical guide to organizing media education in school written by Kruger and Wall (see *The Media Pack* above).

Media at Work, Team Video, 2 Ridgemount Road, London NW2 2QX

This group has produced several video tapes with accompanying notes aimed at student groups, for example, *The British Media*, *Making News* and *Sheer Filth*. Their current catalogue will give further details.

The Media Centre, South Hill Park, Bracknell, Berkshire RG12 4PA

This centre organizes training in media and video for teachers, publishes teaching materials and organizes conferences and courses. It publishes a termly magazine, *Media Education*, which includes articles and practical activities. It has also produced a video about media education in the primary school called *Teaching Media Matters*.

Media Education Development Unit, Scottish Film Council, 74 Victoria Crescent Road, Glasgow G12 9JN

Amongst the resources published by this unit is *Baxters – The magic of advertising* which consists of video and notes for a case study in advertising.

Pagemaker

Pagemaker is a software package for desk top publishing that will run on a BBC computer. It offers a wide variety of fonts, layout possibilities, and graphics (using a mouse), and has a video digitizer facility which can transfer still video shots on to the VDU. *Pagemaker* is published by Advanced Memory Systems Ltd, 166/170 Wilderspool Causeway, Warrington WA4 6QA. This company also produce a program called *Stop Press* for newspaper-style layout.

Pitman, 5 Bentinck Street, London W1M 5RN

In addition to the printed materials published by Pitman, there is a video *Communication at Work* with useful material, particularly for teaching within a business context.

Rank Training, 3 Centaurs Business Park, Grant Way, Isleworth, Middlesex TW7 5QD

Rank Training produce videos and training packages aimed primarily at the 'management training' market and hence the hire or purchase cost is beyond most educational establishments and the focus is fairly specific, e.g. *Basic Sales Skills*. However, if you can obtain them there are some relevant materials on topics such as letter- and report-writing, presentations and meetings, leadership and teamwork.

Routledge Publishers, 11 New Fetter Lane, London EC4P 4EE

Routledge incorporates both Methuen and Comedia which have comprehensive lists of resources essential to the teacher of communication and media. The current catalogue will give details. In this section we are going to mention only four non-book publications from Routledge: *Making Sense of the Media* is a box file of leaflets covering all the major areas of media studies with practical ideas for teaching. The collection was produced by a team from the Communication Studies Degree Course at the Polytechnic of Wales but it is geared towards senior school pupils and college students.

Media Education Journal contains articles by and for media teachers. It is owned and edited by the Association for Media Education in Scotland (AMES), c/o General Education Department, Falkirk College of Technology, Grangemouth Road, Falkirk FIL2 9AD.

The Media Tapes by Andrew Bethell is a series of four videos with accompanying notes on approaches to the study of the mass media primarily aimed at the 14+ age group: Tape 1 *Messages and Meanings* – introduction to the mass media; Tape 2 *Friday the 14th* – on news selection and packaging; Tape 3 *Selling the System* – how advertising works; Tape 4 *The Entertainment Game* – on comedy, quiz shows, etc.

Cultural Studies is an international academic journal published three times a year which particularly focuses on popular culture. It is edited by John Fiske.

Sheffield Media Unit, Central Library, Surrey Street, Sheffield S1 1XZ

This unit publishes materials including a broad-based video – *The Television Programme: How to do media education.*

Somerset Information Technology Unit (SITU), Collinson Centre, Somerset College of Arts and Technology, Wellington Road, Taunton TA1 5AX

SITU has produced learning materials that are suitable for communication groups. These include: a viewdata system called *SomeView* for RM Nimbus, together with supporting materials; guides to using *Communitel*, a BBC viewdata package; and learning material for the desktop publishing packages *Aldus Pagemaker* on RM Nimbus and *AMX Pagemaker (Stop Press)* on the BBC computer. Computer-Assisted Learning (CAL) materials have been developed dealing with basic punctuation and comprehension of texts. These materials can be of use in exploring CAL and its uses in education. A database of English and communications learning materials for post-16 education is being assembled and will be available through the Times Network System. Further information can be obtained from the above address.

TVS – Television South, Community Unit, Southampton SO9 5HZ

TVS Community Unit has produced a pack published by Cambridge University Press entitled *Teaching Television – The Real World*, which consists of (i) a background book providing a context for teaching about TV (e.g. production process, presentation and representation, structure of ITV, advertising, and audience responses), (ii) a video including a programme from *The Real World* popular science series and interviews with the programme team and (iii) teaching notes incorporating lesson plans, worksheets and project ideas.

Timeworks

Timeworks desk top publishing software is a package produced for approximately £100 which runs on a personal computer. It is published by GST, 8 The Green, Willingham, Cambridgeshire CB4 5JA.

Video Arts Limited, Dumbarton House, 68 Oxford Street, London W1N 9LA

Video Arts produce some very witty and well dramatized videos and support materials for 'management training', for example on meetings, selling, using the telephone and so on. Unfortunately the hire and purchase costs are beyond most educational budgets; it may be worth contacting your local industries or training agencies to see if they have copies you might borrow!

Publishers

Most educational publishers produce some publications in the area of English, communication, social skills or media studies. However, the following publishers in particular have a useful list of resources and we recommend you get yourself on to their mailing lists. You will also find other useful references throughout this chapter.

Edward Arnold, 41 Bedford Square, London WC1B 3DQ
Cambridge University Press, The Pitt Building, Trumpington Street, Cambridge CB2 1RP
Heinemann Educational Books Limited, 22 Bedford Square, London WC1B 3HH
Longman Group Limited, Burnt Mill, Harlow, Essex, CM20 2JE
Macmillan Education Limited, Houndmills, Basingstoke, Hampshire RG21 2XS
Routledge, 11 New Fetter Lane, London EC4P 4EE
Sage Publications Limited, 28 Banner Street, London EC1Y 8QE

Organizations and associations

The following addresses include contacts and locations for materials or places to visit.

The Advertising Association, Abford House, 15 Wilton Road, London SW1V 1NJ

Publishes materials useful for students, e.g. a series of students' briefs.

The Advertising Standards Authority, Brook House, Torrington Place, London WC1E 7HN

Produces leaflets and videos about the code of advertising practice, and also a monthly case report of their response to complaints.

The Associated Examining Board, Stag Hill House, Guildford GU2 5XJ

Keeps a list of regional teacher contacts who organize meetings and conferences for communication studies teachers.

Association for Liberal Education, c/o Ken Swallow, People's College of FE, Nottingham

The ALE publishes a regular journal, *Liberal Education*, and occasional papers on aspects of general education and communication. There are also regional meetings and an annual national conference.

Association for Media Education in Scotland, c/o Department of Film and Television Studies, University of Scotland, Stirling

The AMES organizes an annual conference and occasional events.

Association for the Teaching of the Social Sciences, Pineleigh, Silverdale Road, Arnside, Carnforth, Lancs. LA5 0EH

Publishes *The Social Science Teacher* and organizes regional and national conferences.

British Film Institute Education Department, 21 Stephen Street, London W1P 1PI

The BFI organizes conferences, provides an advisory service and maintains a network of regional resource banks as well as publishing materials.

Communication Studies Network

Convenor: Andrew Beck, South Warwickshire College of Further Education, Alcester Road, Stratford-upon-Avon, Warwickshire CV37 9QR. Organizes an annual conference, maintains a regional network of contacts and publishes an occasional newsletter.

Film Education, 37–39 Oxford Street, London W1R 1RE

This organization, funded by the British film industry, publishes a regular newsletter, study guides to films and an industry pack.

Media Studies Resource Centre, Centre for Educational Technology, Civic Centre, Mold, Clwyd CH7 6ND

Produces teaching materials and resources for primary and secondary schools, e.g. *Working Papers for 16+ Media Studies.*

Museum of the Moving Image (MOMI), South Bank, London SE1 8XT

The new museum (opened September 1988) developed by the BFI which tells the story of the moving image from earliest times to the present day, concentrating on cinema and television. Study guides and group visits available.

The National Association of Teacher Educators and Advisors in Media Education (TEAME)

C/o Department of English and Media Studies, University of London Institute of Education, 20 Bedford Way, London WC1H 0AL. A recently formed group which has organized events for this sector.

National Media Education Archive

C/o Film and Video Officer, Portsmouth College of Art and Design, Winston Churchill Avenue, Portsmouth. Formed in association with the BFI to house materials and documents relating to media education. They welcome contributions for the collection, e.g. report of a media education project, student worksheets, teachers' notes, photos, slides, video.

National Centre of Photography, The Royal Photographic Society, The Octagon, Milsom Street, Bath

Permanent and temporary exhibitions of equipment and both historic and contemporary work.

National Museum of Photography, Film and Television, Princes View, Bradford

A branch of the Science Museum and hence a stress on the technical rather than the socio-economic-cultural perspectives. Permanent and temporary exhibitions. Things to do, e.g. be TV newsreader. Impressive IMAX cinema.

Society for Education in Film and TV (SEFT), 29 Old Compton Street, London W1V 5PL

SEFT produces teaching packs, books, journals and a newsletter, *Initiatives*. Amongst the packs particularly useful are the photo sequences, e.g. *The Visit, The Station, The Market*; and a front-page simulation with text and photos for editing, *Choosing the News*.

Women's Media Action and Monitoring Network

C/o Wesley House, 4 Wild Court, Holborn, London WC2 5AX. This group publishes a regular magazine on advertising and media issues, especially sexist stereotyping, and publishes monitoring reports of media output, for example on *Women as Sex Objects*. Worth subscribing.

Chapter seven

Where do communication students go?

We have not sought in this book to justify, or to philosophize about, the teaching/learning of communication in schools or colleges, but rather to describe what communication has come to include and how it can be taught.

We assume that communication, even when it is labelled 'English' or 'personal and social education', is now generally accepted as part of the core curriculum. Communication work develops a range of skills, knowledge, understanding and personal qualities that are necessary for life roles in both social and work contexts. We believe the functioning skills of reading, writing, listening, using non-verbal behaviour, receiving and producing audio-visual media, and using technological equipment are necessary for all. We also believe that the skills require the underpinning of knowledge about people, communication processes, social, economic and cultural issues and personal values.

In this chapter, we are providing a brief guide to how communication skills and knowledge can be useful preparation for a wide variety of general careers that demand people skills, and a cluster of more specialist media-related careers, and also give details of a selection of higher education courses in communication, cultural and media studies.

Does this job require communication skills?

We take it as axiomatic that the ability to understand other people's messages and to express oneself are essential skills for any job. Obviously, people-based careers – management, administration, personnel, travel, tourism, catering, hairdressing, nursing, social work, teaching, and so on – make particular demands on our ability to communicate and relate to other people. However, technology-based careers – construction, manufacturing, mining, farming, surveying – also demand communication skills and the ability to get

155

on with people. Any business succeeds or fails through its people and its relationship with its customers.

In reviewing advertisements for a variety of jobs, it is striking that 'ability to communicate' occurs very frequently, as in the following examples taken from one national newspaper on one day:

- Are you able to assimilate, analyse, distil and communicate information effectively, both verbally and on paper? Then join a lively team helping one of Britain's biggest industries.
- Your drive and ambition, interpersonal skills and maturity will be allied to a flexible approach demanded in this rapidly evolving environment.
- Degree discipline isn't important. But personality, communication skills, the capacity to expand within a fast changing business – these are all essentials.
- Candidates should hold a degree/HNC in a science or engineering subject and be able to demonstrate an awareness of a sales/marketing environment, together with good communication skills.
- You will need sharp communication skills and the capacity for developing effective business relationships. Maturity, confidence and demonstrated leadership are obviously important.
- The ability to communicate complex issues in a cogent and coherent manner is essential.
- You are forceful, but diplomatic, able to use your fluent communication skills effectively at all levels.
- You need proven oral and written ability to communicate with non-technical staff.

These extracts from advertisements were taken from a wide range of different posts in selling, management, trade union, charity and engineering businesses.

Specific communication and media careers

Print, radio, and television journalism, broadcasting, performing, film, advertising, art and design, publishing, and so on are all career areas that demand specific communication and media skills and knowledge. Within these occupational areas there are many specific jobs from reporter to editor, camera operator to director, script writer to production assistant, advertisement copy writer to account manager, researcher to performer.

There are many books and booklets on all these careers with details of personal qualities, experience and qualifications they require. Since almost all of these occupational areas are perceived by many people to be 'glamorous', there is strong competition for positions, and whilst some jobs in the media industries are highly paid, others are not.

Film and TV: The way in by Robert Angell (1988, BFI) gives information on how the industry is organized, what the various jobs involve, what qualifications are required and how to set about making an application. The Careers and Occupational Information Centre (COIC), Moorfoot, Sheffield S1 4PQ, publishes a range of career guides including *Journalism* and *Media*.

In the next section of this chapter, we shall mention some courses which provide training for careers in the media. However, it is beyond the scope of this book to give full details of such careers and courses and we refer you to your careers service library for details. The British Film Institute publishes a booklet every few months, *Directions*, which lists practical short training courses in video and film available in each region of the UK.

Higher education courses at colleges, polytechnics and universities

Twenty years ago, virtually no courses under the name of communication studies, media studies, or cultural studies existed. Additionally, there were very few film studies or practical production courses at that time. Now it is very different. A wide range of opportunities to study these areas across a spectrum from vocational production skills to theoretical academic approaches is available. The interdisciplinary discipline of communication is now established in higher education.

This section will give a listing of communication studies and related courses at higher national diploma and first degree level which reflect the range available. Since new courses are currently being developed, this list cannot be totally comprehensive, and we have selected only those courses that have a significant communication studies content. We have not tried to include all courses which contain some communication work: for example, at the academic end of the spectrum, many sociology and psychology courses include communication issues; in a more practical sphere, many art and design courses will include communication and media practice; and many business and management studies courses will also include elements of communication which may be labelled 'advertising' or 'public relations'; and elsewhere performing arts courses including drama, film and television will include communication and media work.

The British Film Institute publishes two guides to film and media studies in higher education which survey those specific courses: first, *Film and Television Training* – undergraduate and postgraduate courses with emphasis on practical work; and second, *Studying Film and TV* – higher education courses which include study of film and TV. There are also a number of general reference books which are useful and can be obtained from your local careers service office or your school or college career library. These include:

Which Degree vol. 1, Arts, Humanities, Language published by the New Point Publishing Company, London.
University Entrance – The Official Guide published by the Association of Commonwealth Universities.
Polytechnic Courses Handbook published by the Committee of Directors of Polytechnics.
A Compendium of Advanced Courses in Colleges of Further and Higher Education published by the London and South Eastern Regional Advisory Council for Further Education.
CNAA Directory of First Degree and Diploma of Higher Education Courses, published by the Council for National Academic Awards.
Survey of Polytechnic Degree Courses published by Careers Consultants Limited.
The CRAC Degree Course Guide, published by CRAC, Cambridge.
Degree Courses Offers, published by Careers Consultants Limited.
Colleges and Institutes of Higher Education Annual Guide, published by the Standing Conference of Principals.

We have prepared an alphabetical list of institutions in three sections: colleges, polytechnics, and universities. For each institution, we shall list the communication and media studies courses available for degree or higher national diploma with an indication of the course content. We have not attempted to give details of specific entry requirements for each course because they are generally similar. The *minimum* entry requirement for all higher national diploma courses is five subjects at GCE or GCSE grade C or above including one subject at A level. For degree courses, five subjects at GCE or GCSE at grade C or above, including two at A level. These are minimum requirements and in most cases more than this minimum is required. GCSE English is normally a requirement and a wide range of A-level subjects is acceptable. Some institutions suggest favoured subjects are communication studies, English, economics, modern languages, history, sociology, or psychology. However, the arts, social sciences and natural sciences are all usually acceptable. BTEC diplomas and the International Baccalaureate offer an alternative to A levels.

Many courses welcome mature students (usually defined as over twenty-one or over twenty-three) on to their courses on the basis of their relevant experience and potential to follow the course. Local colleges often offer 'access' courses to help mature students obtain entry to higher education without taking the traditional A-level route.

With regard to the content of courses, we have only included a general flavour of the areas of study. It is necessary to refer to the college prospectus or the course leaflet to obtain details of the content and the options within courses labelled as 'Communication Studies'. Courses with the same title can, of course, vary considerably. Usually, however, these courses will include some practical work (video, print, film, radio) and some sociology, psychology and linguistics. Although practical work sometimes includes work placements, degree courses in communication studies should not be seen as providing training for a media career. The authors of *Which Degree* put this quite bluntly, 'Degrees in this field may sound glamorous and interesting, but at the same time, their titles give the prospectus browser little idea of what might be involved when they get through the departmental portals. What these courses certainly are not, are training courses for exciting jobs in television, advertising or Fleet Street'.

But having given that health warning, we believe that as teachers of communication, it is useful to know that committed students now have an interesting range of opportunities to study at first degree, higher national diploma and postgraduate level. We have not tried in this book to provide information about postgraduate diplomas and courses, but most of the institutions which are listed in the following pages also provide postgraduate work. In addition to these, a number of other British universities offer postgraduate work in communication, media and drama but do not offer first degrees.

Courses listed below are full-time unless indicated otherwise.

Colleges

Bangor Normal College (Y Coleg Normal), Bangor, Gwynedd, LL57 2PX

BA Combined Studies (Communication) (three years)
To prepare students for bilingual situations in Wales to work in management, local government or mass media. Combines academic and vocational elements.

Where do communication students go?

Bournemouth and Poole College of Art and Design, Wallisdown Road, Poole, Dorset, BH12 5HH

HND in Film and Television (two years)
A professional standard course leading to specialization in camera, editing, sound and production.

Bulmershe College of Higher Education, Woodlands Avenue, Reading, RG6 1HY

BA Combined Studies (three years)
Film and Drama are available as major or minor study areas alongside a wide range of other subjects.

Canterbury Christ Church College, Canterbury, Kent, CT1 1QN

BA/BSc joint honours degree including Radio/Film/TV Studies (three years)
A wide range of other subjects is available (Art and Design, English, Geography, Maths and Computing, Movement Studies, Religious Studies, Science).

Year 1 – development of sound broadcasting, techniques of radio production, history of film, technical skills;
Year 2 – critical studies in either radio or film, or TV, plus option from documentary, fiction or animation;
Year 3 – further specialization in second-year subjects.

Dorset Institute of Higher Education, Wallisdown Road, Poole, Dorset, BH12 2BB

BA Honours in Communication and Media Production (three years)
Covers academic, practical, aesthetic, technical and professional aspects of work in the media. First year, broad foundation with late specialization in audio, video, or computer graphics leading to major production in third year. Six-week professional attachment to media institution.

BA Honours in Combined Studies (three years)
Choose the study areas from Communication Processes, Decision-making Processes, Computer-based Information Systems (one Law). Prepares students for careers in management, the professions and public services.

Glasgow College of Technology, Coweaddens Road, Glasgow, G4 0BA

BA Communication Studies (three years)

Year 1 – Mass   Communications,   economics,   psychology,

160

sociology, practical studies;
Year 2 – Mass Communication and Society, media analysis, social psychology and communication, marketing, quantitative methods, practical studies;
Year 3 – Impact of mass communications; media, culture and society; marketing, interdisciplinary services, media analysis, practical studies.

Gwent College of Higher Education, Faculty of Art and Design, Clarence Place, Newport, Gwent, NP9 OUW
BTEC HND in Film and TV Practice (two years)

Year 1 – basic film and television theory, pre-production design, animation, video, computer;
Year 2 – students specialize in one or possibly two of the following areas: Camera, Editing, Sound, 2D animation, 3D animation, Rostrum Operation.

Harrow College of Higher Education, Watford Road, Northwick Park, Harrow, Middlesex HA1 3TP
BA Honours in Photography, Film and Video (three years)
Choose from a variety of subjects: Culture and Communication, History and Theory of Media, Information Technology, Mass Media Studies. Gain knowledge of equipment, materials and processes used in photography, film and radio.

Kent Institute of Art and Design, Maidstone College of Art and Design, Oakwood Park, Maidstone, ME1 8AG
BA Honours Communication Media
There are 'pathways' in Design Communication, Illustration and Time-based Studies. The Time-based Media 'pathway' concentrates on radio/TV production.

London College of Printing, Elephant and Castle, London, SE1 6SB
BA Media Production and Design (four-year sandwich)
Includes visualization and design for publishing, information design, design for broadcasting and audio-visual production, practical work, information and cultural studies, cultural history, business studies for media industry, placements in media.

BA Film and Video (three years)
Techniques, materials, equipment of sound and image production; film and video theory; historical analysis; study of contemporary culture. The London College of Printing also offers higher national

diplomas in related areas of media and journalism.

Napier Polytechnic of Edinburgh, Colinton Road, Edinburgh, EH10 5DT
BA Photographic Studies (three years)
Includes photographic studies, communication studies, audio-visual media, graphic design, historical studies, business studies. Emphasis on visual expression and communication and on professional skills.

The National Film and Television School, Beaconsfield, Bucks, HP9 1LG
The NFTS provides three-year full-time short courses in all aspects of film and TV production: animation, art direction, camera, direction, documentary, editing, music composition, production script, sound, but note that it only accepts 'mature' students.

North Cheshire College, Padgate Campus, Fearnhead, Warrington, WA2 0DB
BA Honours in Media and Communication Studies with Business Management (validation by University of Manchester) (three years)
Combines units of Business Management, Information Technology, and Media Studies with specialist units in TV, Video, Sound, Print Media, Photography, Film, Publishing. Strong emphasis on practical work.

Queen Margaret College, Clerwood Terrace, Edinburgh, EH12 8TS
BA Communication Studies (three years)
Includes interpersonal/organizational/mass communication skills; culture and communication and social institutions; social influence; information studies; television representation; individuality and interaction; industrial society.

College of Ripon and York St John, York Campus, Lord Mayor's Walk, York, YO3 7EX
BA/BSc Combined Studies (validated by University of Leeds) (three years)
Drama, Film and TV can be combined with a range of other subjects.

Trinity and All Saints' College, Brownberrie Lane, Horsforth, Leeds, LS18 5HD
BA in Communication and Public Media (three years)
Combines an academic study from a wide list including Communication and Cultural Studies, with a professional study in Public Media. Placement in media industry.

Watford College, Hempstead Road, Watford, WD1 3EZ

Diploma in Advertising Writing (one year)
In addition to copywriting, topics covered include media, marketing, direct marketing and introduction to video, TV and radio production. Watford College also offers courses in Publishing, Business Studies (Advertising and Marketing) and Visual Communication.

Polytechnics

City of Birmingham Polytechnic, Perry Bar, Birmingham, B42 2SU

BA Hons Communication Studies (three years)
Theoretical and practical approaches to communication with particular reference to the media. Core units in Communication Theory, including historical and sociological perspectives, with units on Professional Writing, Radio, Video, Photography and Media and Arts Promotion. Two-month industrial placements. 25 per cent of the course consists of a second subject area chosen from English, Sociology, Economics and Government.

Bristol Polytechnic, Coldharbour Lane, Frenchay Lane, Bristol, BS16 1QY

BA or BA Hons Humanities (three years)
Modular course with option to specialize in Communications and Cultural Studies alongside wide range of humanities and social science units.

Coventry Polytechnic, Priory Street, Coventry, CV1 5FB

BA Hons Communication Studies (three years)

Year 1 – Media Studies, Workshop, Introduction to Sociology, Studying Cultures, Psychology of Communication, Development of Press and Broadcasting.
Year 2 – Psychology of the Social Individual, Sociology of Mass Communication, Language, Culture and Communication, Research Methods, and two from: Advertising, Film Studies, Design, Art, Photography, Analysis of Media Organizations; or option exchange of one term with French or Belgian university;
Year 3 – Mass Communication: Social and Cultural Perspectives, Ideology, Politics and Communication, Extended Essay, and three from: Popular Forms in Film and Television, Contemporary Art, Media Policy, Information Structures, Journalism.

Liverpool Polytechnic, Rodney House, 70 Mount Pleasant, Liverpool, L3 5UX

BA/BA Hons/Dip HE Integrated Degree including Media and Cultural Studies (three years)
Media and Cultural Studies is a second and third year option including units from Theory and Methods, British Culture and Industrialization; Mass Communications; Popular Culture; TV Drama; Film Studies; Press and TV; Journalism; Popular Literature.

Polytechnic of Central London, 309 Regent Street, London, W1R 8AL

BA Hons Media Studies (three years)
Equal combination of academic and practical study.

Year 1 – academic: Mass Media Institutions and their Publics; Media Analysis; practical: Skills of Print, Journalism, Radio and Video.
Year 2 – academic: Introduction to Social Theory; Political and Social Context of British Mass Media; Analysis; practical: Print Journalism or Radio or Video.
Year 3 – academic: Contemporary Media Policy and Theories; practical: Print Journalism or Radio or Video.

North-East London Polytechnic, Romford Road, London, E15 4LZ

BA Hons Cultural Studies (three years)
This course develops ways of making sense of the society we live in through a study of English culture from the seventeenth century. In year 2 (mainly nineteenth century) and year 3 (mainly twentieth century) students choose one cultural form from Literature, Philosophy, Popular Culture, together with core studies in History and Cultural Theory.

Polytechnic of North London, Holloway Road, London, N7 8DB

BSc Hons Applied Social Science Modular Scheme: Information and Communication (three years)
This modular scheme consists of five 'pathways', one of which is Information and Communication. This 'pathway' develops theoretical insights and practical competence in three broad interrelated fields: information technology, librarianship and mass communications. Includes short placements in relevant information and communications agencies.

Manchester Polytechnic, All Saints, Manchester, M15 6BH

BA Hons Design for Communication Media (three years)

Students will be expected to have taken an Art and Design foundation course. There are six main related areas of study: Advertising: range of conceptual skills with aim of becoming copywriters and/or art directors in advertising agencies; Graphic Design: skills relating to information and publicity design, packaging and editorial design; Illustration: students with high levels of draughtsmanship develop these with aim of becoming freelance illustrators; Photography: appreciation and uses of still photography leading to production of individual portfolio; Design for Learning: use of graphic design, illustration, photography, and TV related to design and production of materials for use in education and industrial training; Film/Television: experience in film, television and sound production, script writing, set design, photography, animation and slide/tape design.

Middlesex Polytechnic, Trent Park, Cockfosters Road, Barnet, Herts, EN4 0PT
BA Hons Contemporary Cultural Studies (three years)
This is a final-year study as part of a modular degree scheme. It examines cultural theory as developed over the pasty forty years within British cultural history. Culture is broadly defined as encompassing, for example, visual languages education, youth sub-cultures, as well as cultural 'artefacts' such as films and television. Issues of culture and ideology are central questions with particular attention to gender, class, and race within contemporary British culture.

Newcastle-upon-Tyne Polytechnic, Ellison Building, Ellison Place, Newcastle-upon-Tyne, NE1 8ST
BA Hons Media Production (three years)
Students need to have done an Art and Design foundation course and to have five GCE/GCSE subjects or three GCE/GCSE plus one A level. There are five areas to the course: Media Theory, Photography, Film and Video, Production Research, and Motion Graphic Design. Students study all five areas, then proceed to specialize in one of the four practical areas.

Portsmouth Polytechnic, Ravelin House, Museum Road, Portsmouth PO1 2QQ
BA Hons Cultural Studies (three years)
Concerned with analysis of culture and society with special reference to Britain. Year 1 – introduction to methods of literary criticism, history and sociology, presented through twentieth-century materials; Years 2 and 3 – cover theories in cultural analysis linked to key themes in nineteenth- and twentieth-century culture and society. Options include films, popular fiction and the media.

165

Plymouth Polytechnic, Drake Circus, Plymouth, PL4 8AA

BA Combined Hons Arts or Humanities
There are choices for major and minor subjects which include an option in Media.

Sheffield City Polytechnic, Pond Street, Sheffield, S1 1WB

BA Hons Communication Studies (three years)
Aims to provide a broad understanding of the role of communication in modern society, drawing on knowledge from psychology, linguistics and cultural (literary and media) studies.

Year 1 – interpersonal communication, verbal communication, social processes, sociology of mass communication and a practical workshop. Also descriptive linguistics and popular culture;
Year 2 – language, social identity, ideology, communications technology and practical project work;
Year 3 – Communications theory, prejudice, textual analysis and advanced communication skills.

Sunderland Polytechnic, Langham Tower, Ryhope Road, Sunderland, SR2 7EE

BA and BA Hons Communication Studies (three years)
Integrates aspects of study from sociology, linguistics, psychology and cultural studies; not designed to train practitioners but includes practical work in radio, video and computing.

Year 1 – psychological processes, social contexts of perception, representation and language, popular fiction and TV;
Year 2 – options in visual or verbal communication, culture and gender, computing and information technology. All study products, history and organization of broadcasting and the press, some linguistics and psychology;
Year 3 – options in representations of women in fine art, photography and film; fiction; language; advertising and public relations; popular culture, and the language of films. All study documentary film and television and media audience research.

Trent Polytechnic, Burton Street, Nottingham, NG1 4BU

BA Hons Communication Studies (three years)
Focuses on human communication in contemporary society with emphasis on problems and issues. Draws on literature, sociology, psychology, semiotics and linguistics.

Years 1 and 2 – foundation course in the above disciplines. Year 2 includes brief professional placement and choice of inter-disciplinary units or computing and information technology; Year 3 – all take communication through discourse and problems and issues in contemporary communication. Options to specialize in literature or sociology with broad-based course. Three options from communication, emancipation and the public sphere; mass communications and politics; cultural imperialism; imperialism and literature; Africa; proletarian fiction; the black experience in fiction; advanced topics in the psychology of communication; psycho-linguistics; the craft of writing.

Polytechnic of Wales, Pontypridd, Mid-Glamorgan, CF37 1DL

BA Hons Communication Studies (three years)
Explores nature and character of communicative practices and 'meaning-making' within society through four overlapping strands of study – culture, society, language, media.

Year 1 –   foundation course in all four strands including practical work and information technology;
Years 2 and 3 –   specialize in three areas of study with practical studies in one of them. These include interaction analysis; syntactic, semantic and discourse analysis; film and video making, television studio production and electronic field production.

Universities

Comparatively few British universities yet offer a single subject honours degree in Communication Studies but a number now offer Communication, Cultural or Media Studies as a subject area in a combined degree or joint honours degree. In the following list we have only provided brief notes about these degree combinations: we recommend you follow up your interests by obtaining the appropriate prospectus and leaflets. These, and other, universities may offer postgraduate courses in aspects of communication but we have not included such information here.

The Queen's University of Belfast, Belfast, Northern Ireland, BT7 1NN

BA Hons Language and Communication (three years)
Integrated course providing a range of concepts and skills in language, science and information technology.

Year 1 –   psychology and computer science usually with

	English and philosophy;
Years 2 and 3 –	include eight set courses, two each from departments of English, philosophy, psychology and computer science.

University of Birmingham, PO Box 363, Birmingham, B15 2TT

BSocSc (Hons) Media, Culture and Society (three years)

This course is available from September 1989 and offers some ways of understanding contemporary culture and society, with a main, though not exclusive, focus on Britain.

Year 1 –	media, culture and society in contemporary Britain; introduction to cultural studies; and three options from: social and economic history; introduction to social sciences; introductory courses on West African societies; and computing;
Year 2 –	theories of culture and ideology; media today: organization, genres, alternatives; gender in contemporary British societies; politics and ideology of race; and one option from a wide range of social, political and international topics;
Year 3 –	a dissertation and four courses from a range including nationalism and national identity; the West Midlands; and social change and development in Latin America.

Birmingham University also offers combined honours and general honours degrees which include media and cultural studies.

University of Bradford, Bradford, West Yorkshire, BD7 1DP

BA Hons Communications (Interdisciplinary Honour Studies) (three years)

Year 1 –	human nature (through philosophy and psychology) and human society (through literature and sociology);
Year 2 –	science, ethics and religion;
Year 3 –	dissertation and seminars: two from philosophy, psychology, sociology, literature and communication.

Brunel University, Uxbridge, Middlesex UB8 3PH

BSc Communication and Information Studies (four-year sandwich)

Years 1–2 –	sociology, psychology, economics or law, computing and information technology, video and mass communications, project work in computing and video;

Years 3–4 – theory, application and management of new communication and information technologies; social, psychological, economic and legal contexts; language, communication and information. Continuing project work. Three work placements.

University of East Anglia, Norwich, NR4 7TJ
BA Hons Films and English Studies (three years)
Aspects of literature, history, philosophy or linguistics as foundations, plus choice of options including English/American Studies; Medieval Literature and History; European Romanticism; Seventeenth Century; Drama and Literature. Then choice of courses from British cinema and TV and their relation to twentieth-century history and culture; World War II and cinema; history of TV. A dissertation and practical film/video project.

University of Glasgow, Glasgow, G12 8QQ
MA Joint Hons (three years)
Film/Television Studies can be combined with Sociology, English and History of Art. It includes the place of cinema and TV in twentieth-century culture, techniques of analysing films, major theories of film narrative and realism, and institutional forms of British TV. There is also a substantial practical element for joint honours degrees.

University of Kent at Canterbury, Canterbury, Kent, CT2 7NZ
BA Hons The Visual and Performed Arts (three years)
Academic study of the arts for potential careers in arts administration or journalism in the arts. Two core courses: 'Reading the Image' – theoretical problems in the visual art of the west from Renaissance to now and 'Patronage and cultural organization in twentieth-century Britain' – concerned with funding of the arts. Remainder of course includes theory and history of art and either film studies or drama.

BA Hons Communication and Image Studies
Four interdisciplinary core courses: Communications and Culture; Reading the Image; Media, Culture and Society; History and Theory of Imagery, along with option courses from specialized degree programmes in film studies, art history, drama, philosophy, sociology, linguistics, computing, politics, etc. It is not a technical vocational course.

BA Combined Hons (three years)
One may combine Film Studies with English, Drama, Computing,

Comparative Literature, or Classical Civilization.

University of Lancaster, University House, Lancaster, LA1 4YW

BA Hons Human Communication (three years)

Year 1 – a study of the common ground between linguistics, psychology and sociology;

Years 2 and 3 – core courses: language acquisition, meaning and symbol, language in society. Human communication research project. Wide range of options including Social Psychology, Media Sociology, Interpersonal Communication, Language, Ideology and Power.

University of Leeds, Leeds, LS2 9JT

BA Hons Sociology and Cultural Studies

Year 1 – introduction to sociology and to cultural studies; trends of nineteenth and twentieth centuries;

Year 2 – approaches to sociological theory; social processes and institutions; theories of culture;

Year 3 – sociology of knowledge; three options from a list, e.g. sexual divisions and society; contemporary sociological theory; sociology of science.

University of Liverpool, PO Box 147, Liverpool, L69 3BX

BA Hons English and Communication Studies (three years)
Communication Studies can be a combined honours subject with a range of other subjects. Communication Studies draws on a range of theories and methods in order to pose questions, for example, on the nature of visual communication, the formation of public communications policy, or ways in which talk is a part of social interaction. Analysis of language and image and the history of particular communicational forms are parts of the course.

University of London Goldsmith's College, New Cross, London, SE14 6NW

BA Hons Communication Studies only as a subject in combination with others (e.g. sociology) (three years)
Language, experience and behaviour, including psychology, linguistics, semiological analysis of communication; technology, culture and society. Practical work includes film; graphic design; computer graphics; photography; radio; TV; video.

University of Stirling, Stirling, FK9 4LA

BA/BA Hons Film and Media Studies (three years)
First part of course includes elements of communications; authorship in cinema; culture, media and society. Second part of course includes media theory – mass communication and problems of text. Also options for example in advertising, journalism and press; TV and radio drama. Students studying film and media studies and modern language may spend a year abroad.

University of Sussex, Sussex House, Falmer, Brighton, BN1 9RH

BA Hons English with Media Studies (three years)

Year 1 – preliminary course with topics such as language and linguistics; approaches to English studies; introduction to media studies; texts and perspectives;

Year 2 – TV and film analysis; Shakespeare or English special subject or the British press;

Year 3 – period of English literature and further media studies, e.g. images of childhood, popular culture, studies in feminism.

University of Ulster, Coleraine, County Londonderry, Northern Ireland, BT52 1SA

BSc Hons Human Communication (three years)

Year 1 – introduction to psychology of communication, to linguistics and sociology of communication, biology, practical communication, communication on industrial society;

Year 2 – cognition and perception, semantics, communication and industrial society, research methods, social skills training, practical communication, psycholinguistics, discourse analysis, sociolinguistics, social psychology, and work placement in industry; media etc.;

Year 3 – social interaction, written communication, communication in social context, counselling, communication in organizations, project, and one from counselling, social skills, linguistics, etc.

BA Hons Media Studies (three years)
Core of mass media and society; focus on films; TV; radio, press and journalism. Also in year 1 concepts and methods of analysis related to mass media, and in years 2–3 focus on theoretical and practical studies.

University of Warwick, Coventry, CV4 7AL

BA Combined degrees can be taken in *Film and Literature* or *Film and English* (three years)

Year 1 – Film Studies; basic issues and methods;
Year 2 – Forms of narrative; Hollywood and aspects of European cinema;
Year 3 – Film aesthetics; naturalism; special topic in film.

Index

Index